proclamation 2

Aids for Interpreting the Lessons of the Church Year

lesser festivals 3

Saints' Days and Special Occasions

Richard Reid
and
Milton Crum, Jr.

editors: Elizabeth Achtemeier · Gerhard Krodel · Charles P. Price

FORTRESS PRESS   **PHILADELPHIA**

Library of Congress Cataloging in Publication Data (Revised)

Main entry under title:

Proclamation 2.

Consists of 24 volumes in 3 series designated A, B, and C which correspond to the cycles of the three year lectionary plus 4 volumes covering the lesser festivals. Each series contains 8 basic volumes with the following titles: Advent-Christmas, Epiphany, Lent, Holy Week, Easter, Pentecost 1, Pentecost 2, and Pentecost 3.
CONTENTS: [etc.]—Series C: [1] Fuller, R. H. Advent-Christmas. [2] Pervo, R. I. and Carl III, W. J. Epiphany—Thulin, R. L. et al. The lesser festivals. 4 v.
1. Bible—Homiletical use. 2. Bible—Liturgical lessons, English.
[BS534.5.P76]   251   79–7377
ISBN 0–8006–4079–9 (ser. C, v. 1)

8566L80   Printed in the United States of America 1–1365

Contents

Editor's Foreword

The Lesser Festivals 3: Saints' Days and Special Occasions comprise comments on the lectionary assignments for eight festivals from the end of June until the end of September:

St. Peter and St. Paul, Apostles	June 29
St. Mary Magdalene	July 22
St. James the Elder, Apostle	July 25
Mary, Mother of Our Lord (Roman Catholic: Feast of the Assumption)	August 15
St. Bartholomew, Apostle	August 24
Holy Cross Day (Roman Catholic: Triumph of the Cross)	September 14
St. Matthew, Apostle and Evangelist	September 21
St. Michael and All Angels (Roman Catholic: Michael, Gabriel, and Raphael)	September 29

These days are established as Lesser Festivals in the Lutheran calendar. They are observed in the Roman Catholic Church as solemnities, feasts, or memorials, and in the Episcopal Church as Major Feasts. All of them, except Holy Cross Day, commemorate NT figures. St. Michael and All Angels celebrates Michael's preliminary heavenly victory over Satan and his hosts (the occasion of moving the arena of the conflict to earth and human history) and the subsequent role of God's angelic messengers in revelation and human life. Holy Cross Day commemorates the dedication of the Church of the Holy Sepulchre in Jerusalem during the fourth century. It provides an opportunity in the fall of the year to celebrate and proclaim the great Christian symbol of God's revelation of himself.

The other observances focus our attention on persons who followed Jesus during his lifetime. James the Elder is James, the son of Zebedee, brother of John, one of the Sons of Thunder. He is distinguished from James, son of Alphaeus, who shares a feast day with Philip on May 1, and James, the brother of our Lord, who is commemorated in some churches on October 23. Particularly noteworthy for the list in this volume is the appearance of two of the women closest to Jesus: Mary, his mother, and Mary Magdalene.

All of these celebrations entered the calendar of the Western church before the tenth century. The feast of St. Peter and St. Paul, Apostles, is as old as the third century, Holy Cross Day was introduced in the fourth century, and St. Michael and All Angels dates back to the fifth century.

(*The Christian Year*, by Edward T. Horn, III [Philadelphia: Muhlenberg (now Fortress) Press, 1957] provides further information about these festivals, as will any other standard work on the calendar of the Christian year.)

The authors of this volume have experimented with a different format: They have not tried to separate exegetical and homiletical material. The dividing line is often hard to draw, in any case. Instead, they have tried to identify themes which run through the readings for a given day, and invite the preacher to meditate upon those chains of thought using the illumination and guidance provided here. They have tried to make the lectionary readings more lucid and vivid for the individual preacher by providing lexicon definitions of Hebrew and Greek words and by suggesting the literary structure of the readings and how they might relate to each other.

All the lessons appointed in the several lectionaries are considered in this volume. The Lutheran lectionary is the starting point, so these readings often color the interpretations of the others. Within the Lutheran lectionary the authors started with the reading which was most common to the other lectionaries or which most fully elucidated the feast. For each lectionary they have tried to relate its set of readings as coherently as possible so that each preacher need only read the comments on the readings which will be used in his or her liturgy. Thus it is hoped that the volume will be immediately accessible to users in all the traditions represented.

Unless otherwise indicated, Scripture quotations are from the RSV. OT definitions are from the Hebrew Lexicon in Strong's *Concordance* and NT definitions are from Thayer's (Grimm) *Lexicon*.

Milton Crum, Jr., is Howard Chandler Robbins Professor of Homiletics at the Virginia Theological Seminary in Alexandria, Virginia, and author of *Manual of Preaching: A New Process of Sermon Development*. Richard Reid is Associate Dean and Professor of New Testament at the same institution.

Alexandria, Va.   CHARLES P. PRICE

St. Peter and St. Paul, Apostles

JUNE 29

Lutheran	Roman Catholic	Episcopal
Ezek. 34:11–16	Acts 12:1–11	Ezek. 34:11–16
1 Cor. 3:16–23	2 Tim. 4:6–8, 17–18	2 Tim. 4:1–8
Mark 8:27–35	Matt. 16:13–19	John 21:15–19

FIRST LESSON

Lutheran and Episcopal: Ezek. 34:11–16. This reading contains two scenes. The first is that which has been and is. The second is that which will be.

The first scene began on "a day of clouds and thick darkness." The "cloud" is the nimbus or thundercloud; "thick darkness" is gloom, as of a lowering sky. The image of thunderclouds rolling in on us as if to afflict us by their power and confuse us by their darkness should be immediately suggestive of many life situations in both the narrower personal realm and in the broader social arena.

On this cloudy and dark day the people were "scattered abroad." This phrase translates a word meaning "to break apart, disperse, etc." The single word "scattered," in the second half of v. 12, means "to *dash* in pieces, lit. or fig. (espec. to *disperse*)." So the image is emphasized. The people were broken and dispersed. As a society they were attacked and dispersed into exile among peoples and countries of different cultures, values, and religions. As persons they were shattered and they fell apart. They were as a flock of sheep who had become disoriented and alienated from their shepherd and their pasture.

V. 16 summarizes this first scene. The people were "lost" ("to wander away, i.e., lose oneself; by impl., to perish"). They had "strayed" ("been driven away" in some translations). They were "crippled" ("broken," "hurt," or "wounded" in other translations). They were "weak" ("to *be rubbed* or *worn*; hence [fig.] to *be weak, sick, afflicted*"). But some were "fat" ("*greasy*, i.e., *gross;* fig., *rich*") and "strong" ("usu. in a bad sense, *hard, bold, violent*"). The image seems to be one of a greedily aggressive fat pig pushing others away from the trough (vv. 20–21).

Scene two is God's promise of what will be. God himself will be the shepherd who will search for and seek out his sheep. He will "rescue" them (literally, he will "snatch them away") from where they have been scattered. He will bring them back to their own land. The words for land and person derive from the same root. To be brought back to one's land or soil is to be brought back to one's source, to be reconciled to one's roots.

In their own land God will "feed" ("to tend a flock; by extens., to associate with [as a friend]") his people; he will feed them every-where—when they are in solitude on the mountains or in the valleys by the streams (NEB, contra RSV) and when they are with others in inhabited areas. They will lie down with the confident security of an animal who lies down with all four legs folded underneath in "good grazing land" ("*at home*; hence, [by impli. of satisfaction] *lovely*").

God will "bind up" ("to wrap firmly; fig., to rule") the crippled or injured. This image may suggest that God will hold his people together as persons or as a society by the pressure of the demands he places on them. God will "strengthen" ("to *fasten* upon") the weak, who have been rubbed or worn down by pressures, by holding them fast in his steadfast love.

What will God do to the fat and strong? Translations based on the Vulgate, the Syriac Peshitta, or the Septuagint concur with the RSV that God will watch over them. Translations based on the Hebrew Masoretic text say that God will destroy them. While the former might be reassur-ing to those who are fat and strong, the latter seems truer to prophetic witness and to what follows in Ezekiel.

Without distinction, God will feed his people with "justice" ("a verdict [favorable or unfavorable] pronounced judicially"). AV trans-lates "with judgment," which is preferable to RSV's "in justice." Note also "proper food" (NEB).

The Ezekiel reading moves from scene one to scene two in ovine metaphors. By what will the preacher-interpreter be guided in applying the metaphors to human existence (if application is considered to be a part of the hermeneutical-homiletical process)?

One could be guided by Ezekiel's political-social situation in the Exile and ask in what ways are we as a nation or a people with Israel in scene one and, then, what does God's promise in scene two say to us? Or, one could be guided by the other readings for the day. Some different interpretations are suggested in what follows.

FIRST LESSON

Roman Catholic: Acts 12:1-11. This reading contains two scenes similar in mood to that of the Lutheran and Episcopal lesson.

In scene one, Herod attacked the church, killed James the Elder, arrested Peter and imprisoned him with the intent of a later trial and probable execution. "But earnest prayer was made to God by the church" ("prayer *stretched out* with *intentness* of mind").

Scene two took place on the night before the intended trial, at a time when prayer must have seemed futile and when hope must have appeared vain. At this moment, at the brink of human hopelessness, Peter was marvelously rescued. However the rescue may have been observed through ordinary eyes, what happened was so unexpected and wondrous that in the eyes of faith it was God's angels who rescued Peter. Deliverance came as sheer gift, as amazing grace, for neither Peter nor the church could achieve it by their own merits or power.

The Acts reading moves from the imprisonment of scene one, with impending condemnation and death, to the marvelous deliverance of scene two. By what will the preacher-interpreter be guided in applying this story to oneself and to one's church (if application is considered to be a part of the hermeneutical-homiletical process)?

One could be guided by the situation of the church in Jerusalem under Herod and ask in what ways are we as individuals persecuted with Peter or in what ways are we as a church persecuted with the church of scene one? What promise does God's rescue of Peter imply for us in the ability to withstand opposition? One also could be guided by the other readings for the day. Some different interpretations are suggested in what follows.

SECOND LESSON

Lutheran: 1 Cor. 3:16–23. In this lesson there are two movements, either of which could serve as a guide for applying the Ezekiel reading or as a basis for a whole sermon independent of Ezekiel's metaphors.

In vv. 16–17, the implied movement is from not knowing something to knowing it, for Paul would not have had occasion to write what he did unless there had been a problem of not knowing. Knowing sometimes refers to a deeply personal and committed relationship between subject and object—a phenomenon tantamount to faith, and Paul's passionate question suggests that he has this kind of knowing in mind.

The implied not knowing has to do with what God will do and with who the readers are. Readers, of course, include us. First, Paul seeks to move the reader from not knowing who "you are":

(a) From not knowing that "you (as a corporate body or as individual bodies, or as both together) are God's temple" ("used of the temple at Jerusalem, but only of the sacred edifice [or sanctuary] itself, consisting of the Holy place and the Holy of Holies").

(b) From concomitantly not knowing that you are "holy" ("*set apart for God, to be, as it were, exclusively his*").

(c) From not knowing "that God's spirit dwells in you." ("Spirit" refers to "*God's power and agency* . . . , *manifest in the course of affairs*.")

Second, the movement is from not knowing that "if any one destroys

God's temple, God will destroy him.'' ("In the opinion of the Jews, the temple was corrupted, or 'destroyed,' when anyone defiled or in the slightest degree damaged anything in it, or if its guardians neglected their duties; . . . God will destroy such a destroyer by 'punishing him with death.'")

The purpose of these two verses is to direct the reader from not knowing to knowing these things. The verses might serve as a focus to guide the preacher into the meditative interpretation by which the text can be presently applied. In what ways have the preacher, members of the congregation, and the church collectively been guilty of not knowing who we are and so engaged in self-destructive behavior? In what ways do others threaten to destroy the church collectively or as individuals? What is the message of judgment and of hope implicit in the affirmation that God will destroy those who destroy his temple?

In vv. 18–23, the movement is from deceiving oneself to understanding authentic wisdom.

Judging by Paul's other uses of the word, to "deceive oneself" suggests luring oneself from the true doctrine of Christ to a false doctrine, which in this instance is probably a self-righteousness based on human achievement.

Those who deceive themselves think that they are "wise in this age," that is, they think that they know how to survive and succeed in the realm of human activity. Such persons possess the "wisdom of this world," that is, the techniques and strategies which the world offers for making things right for them. This kind of wisdom is marked by a "craftiness" (or "cunning") in behavior. (In the Gospel account of Peter's desire for a messiah exempt from suffering we will see an example of the "wisdom of this world" at work.)

But, actually, the wisdom of this world is "folly" ("because such a man neglects and despises what relates to salvation"). God "catches" those who practice it, as a policeman catches a thief who tries to steal. God knows that "the thoughts of the wise are futile" (*"useless, to no purpose* . . . , leading away from salvation; of heathen deities and their worship, e.g., Ezek. 8:10; 13:6–9, Septuagint").

Paradoxically, the way to authenticate wisdom is by becoming intentionally what the wisdom of this world actually makes one: a "fool"—that is, a person who gives up claiming to be wise, humanly speaking. Persons who do so are open to receive, as gift, what they had been grasping for: for "all things are yours" already—persons, the world, life or death, the present or the future—"all things are yours; and you are Christ's; and Christ is God's." Therefore, boasting based on human wisdom or achievement is out of order.

These verses offer other potential foci for application of Ezekiel's metaphors. In what ways have the preacher, the congregation, or our society strayed into self-deception by trying to grasp through the strategies of worldly wisdom that which can only be received as gift by God's promise? Which of the "all things" God has given us, if proclaimed as gospel, might move hearers from the "craftiness" and "futility" of the "wisdom of this world"?

On this feast, it would be appropriate to meditate on either of the two movements in this Pauline reading in relation to St. Paul's conversion and apostleship. In terms of vv. 16–17, Paul was converted from seeing the building at Jerusalem as God's temple to seeing persons as God's temple, and thus to seeing the value and dignity of persons based on God's grace, rather than on human achievement.

In terms of vv. 18–23, Paul was converted from his Pharisaic self-deception and boasting to giving up his claims to wisdom for Christ (cf. 1 Cor. 4:10) and then was given the authentic wisdom which is "Christ . . . the wisdom of God" (1 Cor. 1:24).

SECOND LESSON

Roman Catholic and Episcopal: 2 Tim. 4:1–8, 17–18. Both the Roman Catholic and Episcopal lectionaries take the Second Lesson from 2 Timothy 4, and they overlap in vv. 6–8, so we will address these three verses for possible applications of Ezekiel's metaphors or the reading from Acts. In scene one, Paul is "already being poured out as a libation" (the JB, more accurately than the RSV), and Timothy is having to "endure suffering" (v. 5). Scene two promises "the crown of righteousness."

Paul applies the OT image of the drink-offering to himself as one whose life is being poured out in service to God. Now the time of his "departure" from this life to the "heavenly kingdom" (v. 18) has arrived. (It is "a metaphor drawn from loosing from moorings preparatory to setting sail.")

The "good fight he has fought." Here "good" means "*excellent in its nature and characteristics, and therefore well-adapted to its ends.*" "Fight" denotes "any struggle with dangers, annoyances, obstacles, standing in the way of faith, holiness, and a desire to spread the gospel." The fighting itself ("fought") is a reference meaning "fig. *to contend, struggle, with difficulties and dangers* antagonistic to the gospel." The "race he has finished" stands for, "in the NT fig., *the course of life* or *of office.*" To "finish" means "*to perform, execute, complete, fulfil* (so that the thing done corresponds to what has been said, the order, command, etc.)."

The "faith he has kept." Faith: "in reference to Christ, it denotes *a strong and welcome conviction* or *belief that Jesus is the Messiah*

through whom we obtain eternal salvation in the kingdom of God."
Kept: "*to hold firmly . . .* as a mental deposit."

In Ezekiel's metaphors, Paul, as a sheep in exile in this present age, has been true to God the Shepherd. Now his deliverance is couched in terms of his being poured out as a libation or drink-offering to God (cf. Lev. 23:13, 18; Num. 28:7, etc.). Presupposed in such an offering is not only the pouring out of one's life, one's blood as symbolized by the wine; the more important presupposition is the merciful God who accepts the offering. In Rom. 12:1, Paul makes explicit the mercy of God as the only justification for offering our lives in service to him and as the only assurance that God will accept our offerings and incorporate them into his good purpose, that is, into eternal life.

This assurance, contained in the drink-offering image, is affirmed in the imagery of scene two. On "that Day" ("*the last day of the present age*, the day in which Christ will return from Heaven, raise the dead, hold the final judgment, and perfect his kingdom") the "Lord (Christ), the righteous judge" (used of God "who executed the laws of his government, and therefore also the law concerning the pardon of sins") will "give me" (with RV contra RSV "award to me," as more consonant with God's acceptance of our offerings as a function of his mercy rather than of our achievement) "the crown ("metaphor: *the eternal blessedness which will be given as a prize to the genuine servants of God and Christ*") of righteousness," ("denotes *the state acceptable to God which becomes a sinner's possession through that faith by which he embraces the grace of God offered to him in the expiatory death of Jesus Christ*"). This crown is already "laid up" ("*reserved for one, awaiting him*") for Paul, and not only for Paul but for all who have "loved" ("denotes *to take pleasure in the thing, prize it above other things, be unwilling to abandon it* or *do without it . . .*; *to welcome with desire, long for*") Christ's "appearing" ("In the NT the 'advent' of Christ—not only that which has already taken place and by which his presence and power appear in the saving light he has shed upon mankind, 2 Tim. i. 10; but also that illustrious return from heaven to earth hereafter to occur, 2 Tim. iv. 8").

The clues in these verses might be followed for application of today's readings. In what ways do you, the preacher, and your congregation "endure suffering" with Timothy or are "being poured out" with Paul in the "fight" or the "race" of living? What is there in the promise of the "crown of righteousness" which might enable you to fight the good fight, finish the race, and keep the faith with Paul?

GOSPEL

Lutheran: Mark 8:27–35 and Roman Catholic: Matt. 16:13–19. There is an intended movement in these readings, but it is not effected for Peter until after the resurrection (as recounted in John 21:15–19, the Gospel reading in the Episcopal lectionary).

Peter is thinking in man's way rather than in God's way (JB, more accurately than RSV). "Thinking" here means "*to direct one's mind to a thing, to seek* or *strive for,*" hence thinking in God's way means "to be intent on promoting what God wills (spec. his saving purposes)" and "thinking in man's way" means "to be intent on what pleases men." (This is an example of the "wisdom of this world" referred to in the Second Lesson.)

In Peter's thinking, "the Christ" must not "suffer," he must not be "rejected," and he must not be "killed" in order to "rise." If such events were to make up the Messiah's story, they would also be included in his disciples' stories. Furthermore, until Peter understood that unless Jesus gave his life "as a ransom for many" all persons would be condemned to die for their own ransoms, the death of Jesus would seem unnecessary (cf. Mark 10:45).

But Jesus said that it was necessary. He "must" ("necessity established by the counsel and decree of God, esp. by that purpose of his which relates to the salvation of men by the intervention of Christ and which is disclosed in the OT prophecies") suffer, be rejected, and be killed. Only then would he be raised up to be seated as King (cf. Acts 2:29–32). So it is with his disciples; the way to glory is the way of the cross. Therefore, Jesus rebuked Peter as he had rebuked the unclean spirit and the stormy wind (cf. Mark 1:25; 4:39).

On this feast day one might ponder in what ways we are sheep who have strayed with Peter into false thinking about Jesus or discipleship and what Jesus' words might say to move us from thinking in man's way to thinking in God's way. The readings suggest that we cannot always rely on human shepherds to lead us in God's way. The Ezekiel reading is preceded by a prophecy against the shepherds of Israel who do not lead their sheep but rather feed themselves. Peter, a shepherd of the new Israel, had himself strayed from God's way to man's way and the "wisdom of this world."

GOSPEL

Episcopal: John 21:15–19. In this reading is found the final scene of the story begun by Peter's confession at Caesarea Philippi which was contained in both the Lutheran and Roman Catholic Gospels. By the time of the resurrection, Peter understood what Jesus had foretold about his death and resurrection and about discipleship. Peter now understood; he loved Jesus and was ready to follow him as Lord. If (in the imagery of the Ezekiel reading) Peter had been in exile from Jesus, Peter was now rescued from exile by the Good Shepherd. If (in the imagery of the 2 Timothy reading) Peter had shunned "being poured out as a libation," Peter had now received enough of the "crown of righteousness" to be able to "endure suffering" as he served as an assistant shepherd to Christ.

In what ways do you, or your congregation, follow Peter away from the exile of disobedience and into the way of the cross? What good news does the crucified and resurrected Good Shepherd bring? How does the "crown of righteousness" which he gives rescue you from exile and enable you, along with Saints Peter and Paul, to follow Christ in obedience to the tasks he lays upon you?

St. Mary Magdalene

JULY 22

Lutheran	Roman Catholic	Episcopal
Ruth 1:6–18 or Exod. 2:1–10	Song of Sol. 3:1–4 or 2 Cor. 5:14–17	Jth. 9:1, 11–14
Acts 13:26–33a		2 Cor. 5:14–18
John 20:1–2, 11–18		John 20:11–18

GOSPEL

Lutheran, Roman Catholic, and Episcopal: John 20:1–2, 11–18. We begin with the Gospel for this feast because it is a reading common to all three lectionaries.

"In the beginning . . . darkness was upon the face of the deep. . . . And God said, 'Let there be light'; and there was light" (Gen. 1:1–3). This was the first day of the "week" of creation.

"Now on the first day of the week (of redemption), while it was still dark ("prop. the darkness due to the want of daylight; metaph. used of ignorance of divine things, and its associated wickedness, and the resultant misery") . . . , Mary Magdalene came to the tomb ("*any visible object for preserving* or *recalling the memory of any person* or *thing; a memorial, monument;* specifically, *a sepulchral monument*") early."

Who was this Mary Magdalene? The only other reference to her in the Fourth Gospel shows that she was one of the three Marys standing by the cross (John 19:25). She also appears in the synoptic passion narratives.

What led Mary Magdalene to stand beneath the cross of Jesus? Who was she and why was she there? Attempts to identify her with any of the other Marys are unconvincing because they are all well distinguished from her. More possible, but still problematical, is the identification of Mary Magdalene as the "woman who had been caught in adultery," a figure who appears in some manuscripts in John, and in others in Luke. She may have been the "woman who was a sinner" in Luke 7:36–50. The probability that either of these unnamed women was Mary Magdalene may depend on the meaning of the one known fact prior to the passion narrative, namely, that "seven demons had gone out" from her (Luke 8:2). (To be afflicted by seven demons seems to indicate the worst of all states, as in Luke 11:26 or in the seven afflictions cited in Deut. 28:22.)

There is no simple answer to the question of Mary Magdalene's culpability for her seven demons. As with the whole of human sin, one is both a victim and a culpable, active agent in the total demonic process. Thus in casting out Mary Magdalene's demons Jesus delivered both a victim and a sinner from the demons which dwelt in her and from the corollary sinful attitudes and actions.

This understanding of demons and culpability gives justification for a tentative identification of Mary Magdalene with the woman taken in adultery, or the woman who was a sinner or, perhaps, both. This identification would make her role in the passion and resurrection narratives as wonderfully unlikely as were the roles of the women in Matthew's genealogy: Tamar (Gen. 38), Ruth, Bathsheba (2 Sam. 11)! It would also explain why she loved Jesus so dearly.

This Mary Magdalene, according to the day's Gospels, came to the place of preserving the memory of Jesus while she was still in darkness about where he really was. She "saw" (Gk. *blepō*, "to perceive by the use of the eyes" and even "when its physical side recedes a purely outward sense") that the stone had been taken away from the tomb. So she ran to tell Simon Peter and the other disciple whom Jesus loved the shocking news that "They have taken the Lord out of the tomb and we do not know where they have laid him." In the omitted vv. 3–10, it is apparent that the two men, even though they are the top-ranking disciples, are of no help. All they do is corroborate Mary Magdalene's assertion by ascertaining for themselves that it was Jesus' tomb and that it was empty.

But back to Mary Magdalene herself. The urgency of her search for the whereabouts of Jesus is manifest in her running and in her stating her problem three times. The identity or motives of the "they" who had taken the Lord away seems irrelevant. What matters is Jesus' *whereabouts*. "We" (the church) do not know where the Lord is. "I" (the individual church member) do not know where the Lord is. If I knew where the Lord was, I would go there and take him away with me. An empty sepulchral monument cannot preserve his memory. I need his body in the tomb.

As Mary "wept" ("to weep audibly, *to cry* as a child") she "stooped to look" ("metaph. *to look carefully into, inspect curiously*") into the tomb; and she "saw" (Gk. *theōreō,* "used primarily of one who looks at a thing with interest and for a purpose") two "angels" ("*a messenger, envoy,* one who is sent"). Mary saw more than the two men had seen, but the presence of the two angels tells the reader that more is going on than a missing corpse, more than even Mary has yet experienced. There is something more to be "seen" before the whereabouts of Jesus can be known. There must be a seeing which goes beyond the two kinds of seeing already experienced.

The content of the something more to be seen appeared to Mary. She "saw" *(theōreō)* what she thought was the gardener. "Woman," he asked, "why are you weeping? Whom do you seek?" The meaning of these words depends on the tone of voice and inflections. The import might well be, "Why in the world are you weeping? Don't you know that the Jesus whom you are seeking is not to be found by preserving his corpse in a tomb in order to preserve his memory? Don't you know that the one you are seeking is alive and is with you wherever you are?" But, if this was the import of the "gardener's" question, Mary missed it, for she was still looking for Jesus' body to remember him by.

Then the denouement! "Mary," Jesus said. He "calls his own sheep by name" (John 10:3). Mary recognized him and her first impulse was to recapture him as he had been in the flesh, but Jesus said, *"Do not hold me."* ("Do not handle me to see whether I am still clothed with a body; there is no need of such an examination.") "Do not hold me, for I have not yet ascended to the Father, but go to my brethren and say to them, I am ascending to my Father and your Father, to my God and your God." Then Mary Magdalene no longer tried to hold onto the Jesus of the past as he had been, but she obeyed her living Lord and went to the disciples, not in a frenetic "running" mode but in the confident "coming" mode used so much in John.

"I have *seen the Lord!*" she announced. Now Mary Magdalene was the angel-messenger of the Lord. She had seen, not as she or the two men had seen before, but with the "seeing" (Gk. *horaō*) which "gives prominence to the discerning mind." This seeing was explained in the Greek perfect tense which here indicates that the Lord whom Mary had experienced in the past was still present and operative in the present even though no longer seen by the physical eye. Before her experience of Jesus, Mary had been seeking the whereabouts of a visible corpse in order to preserve Jesus in memory. Now the question of "where they have laid him" is made moot. Jesus is with her. Jesus is living, present Lord.

What was the significance of Jesus' words to Mary which effected this change in her? He told her where he himself, not his corpse, was; Mary really sought Jesus himself, not information about his remains. Jesus told Mary that he was in the church (considered as a body of believers) and in her individually (speaking to the "we" who do not know where, and the "I" who do not know where). He did this by telling Mary that he was ascending to be with and in the Father. And of this ascension Jesus had previously said, "I will come again and will take you to myself, that where I am you may be also" (John 14:3). And when Thomas protested that he did not know where Jesus was going or the way, Jesus responded, "I am the way, and the truth, and the life" (John 14:6): The "I am" is an eternally present "I am." Wherever one is along the way, Jesus is present. From one perspective, Jesus is with us on earth. From another, Jesus' presence raises us to heaven with him. As one of the saints said, "All the way to heaven is heaven, for Jesus said, 'I am the way'."

Jesus also sends his spirit, the spirit of the truth which is Jesus, and he "dwells with you and will be in you" (John 14:17). That is, Jesus will be in you (John 14:20). If anyone loves Jesus, and, like Mary Magdalene, wants to find him, the Father and Jesus dwell in that person. That is the gospel truth (cf. John 14:23).

Later, in the prayer of John 17, Jesus' going to the Father is intertwined with Jesus' being in his people. Jesus prayed that he would make the Father's name known, and he made the Father's name known as the Father and God of Mary and all his disciples. In the conversation with Mary, what Jesus had prayed for happened: The love with which the Father had loved Jesus was in Mary and so the living Jesus was in her. The missing corpse was no longer a concern. Mary knew where Jesus himself was. He was at once ascended in the Father and present in Mary and his church. Once seven demons had dwelt in Mary. Now it was Jesus who dwelt in her and she in him. It was this marvelous good news that Mary announced to the disciples: "I have seen the Lord (in the *horaō* kind of seeing, with the eyes of faith)."

Before doing the meditative interpretation by which this story can interpret the stories of the preacher and congregation and communicate the presence of the living Lord, the preacher will want to survey the other readings for guiding clues. (Of course, you might well use one of the other readings as the focus for your sermon rather than the Gospel as we have done.) To aid in surveying the other readings, we offer brief comments about them.

FIRST LESSON

Lutheran: Ruth 1:6–18 or Exod. 2:1–10. Vs. 8 of the Ruth reading complements the Gospel. As Ruth dealt kindly with a dead son of God, so the living Lord dealt kindly with her. As Mary Magdalene dealt kindly with the dead Son of God, so the living Lord Jesus dealt kindly with her.

In the verses from Exodus, a daughter of Levi attended the "burial" of Moses in the basket among the reeds. The daughter of Pharoah attended the "resurrection" of Moses from his "burial" to life in the courts of the king from whence he was later to "come again" to deliver his people. There is, therefore, some typological interplay between the two readings, but these similarities only exist up to a point. The analogy should not be forced to connect more than it actually does.

SECOND LESSON

Lutheran: Acts 13:26–33a. This reading expands the theme of Mary Magdalene's announcement about Jesus' resurrection. Vv. 31–32 say in the first person plural essentially what Mary said in the first person singular. Proclamation of this good news should enable both preacher and congregation to share Mary's experience of "seeing" the Lord.

FIRST LESSON

Episcopal: Jth. 9:1, 11–14. Judith's story teases the imagination with a suggestion of what may have underlain Mary Magdalene's "sin." Judith, a beautiful Jewish widow, was setting out to deceive General Holofernes of the invading Assyrian army into believing that she wanted to sleep with him. When he succumbed to her seduction, she would cut off his head and deliver it to the demoralized men of Jerusalem.

Before executing her plan to save Jerusalem from defeat, Judith prayed that the "deceit of my lips" would strike down the Assyrians and for her "deceitful words to be their wound and stripe." Judith was planning to lie and kill—wrong actions according to general ethical norms—as a means of serving God's end. In the lesson, she was in God's presence, praying that he would accept her "wrong" acts and use them to serve his end. Judith was engaged in a "teleological suspension of the ethical" in trustful obedience to the God who sometimes lays tasks upon us which cannot be accomplished by normal means and who in his mercy justifies our "wrong" means by his good ends. Is it possible that this was the case with Mary Magdalene also?

Judith's story also parallels Mary's in that both women witnessed to God's victory over evil and by their witness restored the faith of demoralized men.

FIRST LESSON

Roman Catholic: Song of Sol. 3:1–4. "The Bride's" poem might be seen as parallel to the love of Mary Magdalene for the Lord. She sought him, although not in the city as the bride sought her lover but outside the walls. Like the bride, Mary asked the watchman-gardener the whereabouts of the one she loved. But then the two stories diverge. In Mary's story, the watchman-gardener turned out to be himself the one whom she loved, so it was he who found her and not she him. And, furthermore, Mary did not take Jesus to her mother's house in the flesh. Rather she took his presence in the gospel word to the house where the church was gathered.

In meditating on the passage, one might ask what gospel word would present Jesus so as to engender love for him and entice us to seek him? What gospel word does the risen Lord speak to you and to your congregation which might create in you an experience of him similar to that of Mary Magdalene?

FIRST AND SECOND LESSONS

Roman Catholic: 2 Cor. 5: 14–17 and Episcopal: 2 Cor. 5:14–18. The Gospel is complemented in this reading more fully than in all the others. The "old" Mary Magdalene "has passed away" and, "in Christ, she is a new creation." (Recall the parallel between Gen. 1 and John 20 noted above.) Mary had once regarded Christ from a human point of view (literally, had tried to know him according to the flesh, that is, had tried to know Christ through physically finding and seeing his corpse). Now she regards or knows Christ as the one who for her sake died and was raised. Thus it is the love of Christ, not demons, which now "controls" her ("*to hold together* any whole lest it fall to pieces").

We have suggested, through our interpretation of these readings, meditation on the movement in Mary Magdalene's life, particularly in relation to oneself. In what ways are you and your congregation indwelt by "demons"? Could one such "demon" perhaps be the attempt to preserve memories of the past, so that the living Lord who is with us in the actuality of the present experience is eclipsed? Could another of these "demons" be the need to establish your own righteousness, and a resulting inability to risk doing "wrong" in obedience to the Lord as Judith, and possibly Mary Magdalene, did? Why do you admit the "demon" which dwells in you? What does it appear to do for you? Of what does the living Lord assure you that holds your life together ("controls" you, 2 Cor. 5:14) so that the demon can be cast out as

useless? How would life be different with the demon cast out and with
you more fully aware of the Lord who dwells in you?

St. James the Elder, Apostle

JULY 25

Lutheran	Roman Catholic	Episcopal
1 Kings 19:9–18		Jer. 45:1–5
Acts 11:27—12:3a	2 Cor. 4:7–15	Acts 11:27—12:3
Mark 10:35–45	Matt. 20:20–28	Matt. 20:20–28

GOSPEL

Lutheran: Mark 10:35–45. We begin with this Gospel reading as it, or
its Matthean parallel, is common to all three lectionaries. In the
reading, James and John show that they have not yet understood what
Jesus has told them about discipleship. Jesus has told them that discipleship means denying one's self as a self-concerned self and losing one's
old self in commitment to him and the gospel. Only in this indirect way
can a person's true self be saved (Mark 8:34–35). Again, Jesus had told
the disciples that to be "first" one "must be last of all and servant of all"
(Mark 9:35). To enter the kingdom of God one must receive it as a
little child receives gifts (Mark 10:15). In addition, Jesus had warned
that those who followed his teachings would receive persecutions
(Mark 10:30).

In spite of these teachings and warnings, the sons of Zebedee, James
and John, came forward to Jesus, not in committed discipleship to do
what he asked of them, but with the demand that Jesus do for them
whatever they asked of him. They had reversed the meaning of discipleship. For them, discipleship was *not* finding self—one's value and
purpose—indirectly by the strange route of losing one's self for the sake
of Jesus and the gospel. For them, the route to finding self—the route to
glory—was direct and arrogant. Without apology they were concerned
only with themselves.

Jesus was too wise to lecture the two on the meaning of discipleship.
They needed to see for themselves what he had been saying, so he strung
them along toward a position at which they must face the reality of
Christian discipleship. "What do you want me to do for you?" he asked.
They wanted, in advance of doing their discipleship, an assured grant
that they would sit in the chief seats next to Jesus in his glory. That is,
they wanted to share the limelight with Jesus.

But the reality was that if they wanted his glory, they would have to walk his way, for the way to Jesus' glory is the way of Jesus' cross. So Jesus replied that they did not know what they were asking for themselves. Then, to make it clear what they were in reality asking for, Jesus asked, "Are you able *("to be able, have power,* whether by virtue of one's own ability and resources, or of a state of mind, or through favorable circumstances, or by permission of law or custom") to drink the cup ("In the N.T., of the bitter lot [the sufferings] of Christ") that I drink ("to undergo the same calamities which I undergo")?" "Are you able . . . to be baptized ("metaph. *to be overwhelmed with calamities")* with the baptism ("used trop. of calamities and afflictions with which one is quite overwhelmed") with which I am baptized?" And James and John answered, "We are able."

Two questions are raised by this response. Were James and John, in fact, able, and, if so, what was the source of their ability to undergo overwhelming calamity? Jesus left such questions for later reflection and answered instead in the future indicative: The fact is you will drink a cup of suffering like mine and you will be baptized with calamities like mine.

For the present, Jesus said that what the two disciples had demanded was not his to grant, "but it is for those for whom it has been prepared ("almost equivalent to *have been ordained").*" One does not achieve the places of honor with Jesus either by demanding them or by earning them. True disciples trust God and sit in the seat in life which God has prepared for them.

When the other ten disciples heard the conversation, they began to be indignant at James and John. Jesus, rather than join in this venting of emotions, calmly used the opportunity to teach the disciples the difference between what people generally count as "great" and what he considered "great": "You know that in the world the recognized rulers lord it over their subjects and their great men make them (their subjects) feel the weight of their authority" (NEB). Recognized rulers: "lit. those thinking to rule, who indeed only think so, for actually God rules." Lord it over: *"to bring under one's power, to subject to one's self."* Feel the weight of their authority: *"wield power."*

But in contrast it is not so among disciples. Among disciples, "whoever would be *("shown")* great among you must be your servant, and whoever would be first among you must be slave of all." Servanthood is the status symbol par excellence among disciples. Jesus is not giving game rules by which one makes oneself great by one's achievements, even the achievement of serving as a slave. Rather, he is explaining what enables discipleship. The discipleship of serving as a slave is an outward sign that one has received through faith the greatness and the firstness which God reckons to us as gift. This assurance of greatness in God's sight frees us from trying to achieve greatness by "lording it over" others and enables us to live as servants. So the disciple is recognized as great and first, not by works. It is, rather, that discipleship is a symbol that the status of greatness in God's sight has been received as gift. We see this dynamic in Jesus' ministry.

Jesus' greatness was graciously ascribed to him ("prepared" for him, in terms of his answer to James and John) by the Father at his baptism: "Thou art my beloved Son." Jesus had done nothing to earn or merit this greatness in God's sight. Assured of more greatness than he could ever desire, he had no desire to achieve greatness for himself at the expense of others. Rather, as he said, the Son of man did not come to be served as are the world's "recognized rulers." To the contrary: He came to serve. James and John wanted Jesus to grant them the places of greatness above the others, but Jesus grants his life as a "ransom" for many ("to liberate many from the misery and penalty of their sins").

So James and John wanted Jesus to grant them positions of unique greatness. But it is not for Jesus to grant such greatness. Such greatness is for those for whom God has graciously prepared it prior to their demands or achievements. Rather, Jesus countered that to be shown as great one must serve as a slave. That is, one must be like the Son of man who, having in faith received God's gracious grant of greatness through Baptism, had no desire to be "served" with a further grant of greatness. The Son of man served as a servant-slave and granted his life as a ransom for many.

Reflecting on the Gospel one might ask, In what ways am I, or the people I know, like James? Does my concern for "my gift," that is, for what's in it for me, interfere with my functioning as a genuine disciple, as a genuine person? Have I been demanding a unique greatness for myself? Do I demand that I be first in the eyes of others? Have I been trying to get to glory by a route other than Jesus' way, which includes his cup and his baptism of suffering?

Does the reading suggest good news which might make me and those who hear my sermon more like *Saint* James? What is the glory, the greatness, and the firstness which God gives? Is it not so rich that to demand any other is silly? What does it mean that when we suffer, it is drinking Jesus' cup and being baptized with his Baptism? Does not this being with Jesus in the fellowship of his suffering enable us to walk with him obediently in the way of the cross?

In reflecting on such questions one might look for guiding clues in what else is known about St. James the Elder and in the other readings.

Jesus nicknamed James one of the "Boanerges" ("seems to denote fiery and destructive zeal that may be likened to a thunderstorm") or

"Sons of Thunder" (Mark 3:17). James's thunderous destructiveness was rebuked by Jesus (Luke 9:54–55). Nevertheless, James was part of Jesus' inner circle which also included John and Peter. About A.D. 44 he was slain with the sword by Herod Agrippa I (Acts 12:2). Jesus' prophecy that James would drink "the cup that I drink" and that he would be baptized "with the baptism with which I am baptized" was thus fulfilled. This reference brings us to the Second Lesson in the Lutheran and Episcopal lectionaries.

SECOND LESSON

Lutheran and Episcopal: Acts 11:27—12:3a. Vv. 28–30 seem only tangentially related to St. James. The sending of famine relief to Jerusalem by the disciples might be seen as an example of the serving of which Jesus spoke in the Gospel. As one gives one's goods, one gives one's self (for one's lifetime is invested in one's goods) as a "ransom" from, in this case, famine. If James were a victim of the famine, as he might have been, it would be ironic that one who had earlier demanded a seat of honor was now reduced to dependence on others for basic subsistence. One might ponder how God humbles us when we are proud and how we are, in fact, dependent on him always, for everything—for our subsistence and for our greatness. But God is the dependable one. Through the agencies of nature and humankind he provides our sustenance. Through our Baptism he ascribes to us the greatness of being adopted as royal children of God, our King. From the foundation of such secure subsistence and greatness we are able to send relief to those in need, or even, with St. James, to give our very lives. This latter possibility leads into the other segment of this reading.

In 12:1–3, James was one of the Christians upon whom Herod the king laid violent hands. James is the only one listed as having been killed and his execution is said to have pleased the Jews. This brief account leaves gaps which entice the imagination. Why was James singled out (if he was) and why was his execution pleasing to the populace? Was James still demanding to be honored as great? Was he still aggressively trying to achieve greatness? Did he still desire the destruction of those who did not accept his actions? Had he offended the general population by his demands as he had the other ten disciples? Or, had James been changed? Had he found the greatness he sought as a servant and slave of all for Christ's sake? Had he been such an exemplary and attractive disciple that he was singled out for execution? Was he able to drink the cup and be baptized as willingly as he had said to Jesus he would be?

If one concludes that James had changed, this movement might suggest the movement in the sermon. In what ways are you and your congregation like the old James? What is the good news of the greatness of living as a servant and slave for Jesus' sake which transforms us into more of James the saint?

FIRST LESSON

Lutheran: 1 Kings 19:9–18. This reading about Elijah is rich enough in itself to serve as focus for many sermons, but for this feast we will ask how it might complement the Gospel.

Elijah was like James in that he was looking out for his own interests. He was afraid for his life. Jezebel had threatened to take his life away from him, so Elijah, in fear, had fled to Mount Horeb. He came to a cave and there he lodged ("to *stop* [usually overnight]; by impl. to *stay* permanently; hence [in a bad sense] to be *obstinate* [espec. in words, to *complain*]").

As James had come forward to Jesus who gave his life as a ransom for others, so Elijah went to the place where Moses had offered his life as a ransom for others (Exod. 32:30–32). But Elijah, like James, was not yet ready to offer his life. As James had demanded a place of greatness with Jesus, so Elijah arrogated the greatness of being the only person left in covenant with God: "I, even I only, am left."

Elijah may well have expected God to reply with appreciation and approbation. He, like James, may have expected assurance of greatness without the cup and baptism of suffering and death. But the reply which Elijah got was like a violent thunderstorm. First, there was "a great and strong" ("usu. in the bad sense, *hard, bold, violent*") "wind" (Heb. *ruach*, the primary metaphor of God's power), then there was an "earthquake" (*"vibration, bounding, uproar"*). Next there came (after the storm) "the sound of a gentle breeze" (JB).

In none of this was there an explicit reply to Elijah's arrogant claim. Elijah might have inferred that God was telling him, "You do not know what you are claiming for yourself," but he didn't, for he made the same pretentious claim again. God's reply was explicit this time: If you want greatness, obey me and for my sake serve my anointed ones. Forget your pretentions to unique greatness, for there are seven thousand who are great in their zeal for me.

Elijah must have gotten the message just as James had, for there was no more arrogant standing before God expecting to be honored for his pretended unique greatness. Rather, Elijah departed and did obedient service.

SECOND LESSON

Roman Catholic: 2 Cor. 4:7–15. This reading complements the Gospel in that James was surely one of the "earthenware jars" that held the "treasure" of the "Good News" (JB). Furthermore, the lesson addresses a question which was raised in the Gospel. Jesus questioned the ability (or power) of James (and John) to drink his cup and undergo his Baptism. James asserted that he was able, but we raised the question of the source of such ability or power.

St. Paul says that God places the treasure of his Gospel in earthenware jars like James (and you and me) *to make it clear that such an overwhelming power* (or ability, to communicate the Gospel) *comes from God and not from us.* We are enabled by the power of the Gospel treasure which God has deposited in us to withstand the afflictions, perplexities, persecutions, and being struck down which this reading recounts. We have the Gospel assurance "that he who raised the Lord Jesus to life will raise us with Jesus in our turn." And there is no need to demand the greatness of sitting at Jesus' side, for God will graciously "put us by his side."

FIRST LESSON

Episcopal: Jer. 45:1–5. This reading provides several clues for meditating on the Gospel and for its application. First, like James, Baruch's vocation was to serve as a disciple, and, like James, Baruch was dissatisfied. So Baruch complained to his master, Jeremiah: "Woe is me! for the Lord has added sorrow to my pain; I am weary with my groaning, and I find no rest." Also, like James, Baruch sought great things for himself.

God's reply to Baruch through Jeremiah was similar in tone to Jesus' reply to James. Given the immense import of what God was doing, Baruch must be oblivious to what he is asking. God is bringing an old order to its death as a means of raising up a new order, while Baruch is concerned only with himself and his personal greatness! His true greatness could only be found in losing himself (and thus finding himself) in serving God's great purpose.

Finally, there is a promise to Baruch as there was to James: "I will give you your life as a prize of war in all places to which you may go." (The RSV translation is outstandingly accurate.) It is *God* who will *give* him his *life (nephesh,* used widely both literally and figuratively, e.g. desire, heart, mind, self), and God will give him his life as a "prize of war." A "prize of war" comes as a grace to persons who have given their lives in obedient service. Soldiers whose primary concern is gaining a "prize of war" (that is, their "greatness") will probably never get it. The soldiers whose primary concern is obedient service, even though it entails drinking the cup of pain and sorrow, are given their life as a "prize of war." That is, they are given a prize which they were not even seeking. They are given a prize which is wholly unexpected. The Septuagint captures the image well when it translates the Hebrew with a word meaning *"that which is found unexpectedly, piece of good luck, windfall."*

In what ways are you or your congregation like Baruch and James: complaining, demanding an affirmation of your "greatness" above others? Do you know what you are asking? How does this concern with self appear in the context of the great mission which God has called us to serve? What does God's promise of the unexpected gift, the prize of war, mean for you? What does it say which might free us from self-concern and enable us to find our genuine selves through giving ourselves in obedient service to the tasks which God sets before us?

Mary, Mother of Our Lord
(Roman Catholic: Feast of the Assumption)
AUGUST 15

Lutheran	Roman Catholic	Episcopal
Isa. 61:7–11	Rev. 11:19; 12:1–6, 10	Isa. 61:10–11
Gal. 4:4–7	1 Cor. 15:20–26	Gal. 4:4–7
Luke 1:46–55	Luke 1:39–56	Luke 1:46–55

This day provides us with an opportunity to honor Saint Mary, the Mother of our Lord, on a day that has long been associated with her death or with, as the Eastern tradition calls it, the dormition, the falling asleep of the Blessed Virgin. In the Roman Catholic Church the day is observed as the Feast of the Assumption. In the Lutheran and Episcopal lectionaries the emphasis is on Mary as the representative of Israel from which the Messiah comes, and also as a symbol of the faithful community brought into being by his death and resurrection. While the Roman Catholic Church uses the same Gospel, although in longer form, the other two lessons reflect the different emphasis of that tradition.

FIRST LESSON

Lutheran and Episcopal: Isa. 61:7–11. The lesson is the prophet's (presumably Third Isaiah) interpretation of God's activity concerning his people in exile. It provides an insight into what has happened in Israel and, above all, it holds out the promise of God for forgiveness and restoration. The passage begins with the assertion that instead of shame and dishonor the people will receive "a double portion" and that they will be returned to their land where they will have "everlasting joy." The shame and dishonor of Israel refers to the Exile. Israel has been defeated and made captive. That is a cause of shame, of humiliation.

Exile then can be understood as Israel's "problem." Israel is enslaved. But the point is that this exile, this enslavement, is a result of sin and disobedience. Israel made the mistake of thinking either that God did not care about sin and injustice, or at least that in some way Israel was exempt from punishment because God depended on its existence rather than the other way around. The Exile, the shame and dishonor of Israel, is the judgment of God, a judgment rooted in the very nature of God who loves justice and hates robbery and wrong. The lesson first invites the preacher to reflect on the way the judgment of the Lord is expressed among us. Do we not all, at times, tend to believe that God does not really care? Is there not also a tendency to think that God exists to serve us rather than we him?

But the lesson has only a brief backward glance at the shame and dishonor. The dominant note is one of hope for the future, of forgiveness and restoration. God's promise to Israel is: "I will faithfully give them their recompense, and I will make an everlasting covenant with them." The important point here is that this action too is rooted in the nature of God. The key word is "faithfully." It comes from the Hebrew root which can also mean "truth" and it emphasizes the reliability and the dependability of God. He is faithful to his promises and commitments even when others are not. Therefore he restores his people and will make an everlasting covenant. The prophet sees the result of this restoration as a new role for Israel. They will be "known among the nations" and all the world will recognize and acknowledge that "they are a people whom the Lord has blessed."

The story of the Exile, then, is a revelation of judgment and redemption. Without judgment God would be merely sentimental. Without redemption and restoration human life would be total slavery. If there is no forgiveness we are bound by all our past sins and must, consequently, attempt the hopeless tasks of striving after an impossible perfection and a means of self-justification.

But as the end of the lesson expresses the response of the Israelite to the Lord's promise of forgiveness, so too do we know that, like Israel, we are free from our enslavement. As the Israelite's response was one of joy and exultation, so too do we respond to the "good news" of the Lord's gift of forgiveness.

"He has clothed me with the garments of salvation, he has covered me with the robe of righteousness." The image continues with a reference to a bride and bridegroom. The language suggests that God's gift means a new status. The clothes are given to us not because we deserve them, but to mark the new situation in which God has placed us. Our righteousness is not our own but the covering which the Lord has placed upon us, just as he covered Israel with a new status restoring it to its land. The final verse links God's activity in redemption with nature itself. Just as the earth produces plants, so the Lord will surely fulfill his promise to "cause righteousness and praise to spring forth before all nations."

The OT Lesson sets the basic theme for this day. It speaks of God's dealings with Israel and holds out the promise of future fulfillment, of an everlasting covenant. It speaks of judgment and redemption. The Lutheran and Episcopal Second Lesson, from Galatians, will pick up this theme of judgment and redemption, slavery and freedom, given by the Christ who is "born of a woman." Mary's role then is as the one through whom God works to bring his Son into the world. The common Gospel, the Magnificat, is the exultation of Mary that the fulfillment has come. The song matches the mood of the Isaiah passage, but it also reveals that the fulfillment comes in an unexpected way. The final gift of God is not just a renewed Israel, but a Messiah who turns the world upside down.

FIRST LESSON

Roman Catholic: Rev. 11:19; 12:1–6, 10. The imagery of the Book of Revelation is complex and not always easy to understand. The vision of the "great portent" is appropriate for this day if one assumes that the "woman clothed with the sun" who gives birth to a child is Mary. That is a possible interpretation. There are difficulties with it, however. The chief one is that the birth of Christ is followed immediately by his ascension. An exegesis of Psalm 2 may really underlie this passage. The birth referred to here is not the physical birth of Jesus, but rather his "begetting" as Son and King, an event which is associated with the cross and resurrection. The day of the Messiah's enthronement is the day of resurrection. The imagery then falls more easily into place.

The heavenly struggle depicted here is a metaphor for the earthly struggle between the church and the Roman empire. Christ's death which might appear to be the victory of the powers of evil working through the Roman authorities proves actually to be the victory of God. The dragon (Rome, which sees itself as divine and is therefore demonic) tried to devour the Messiah, but the Messiah is taken up to the throne of God. The woman, the messianic community out of which Christ comes, is also in danger. Perhaps there is a reflection of the idea of a faithful remnant of Israel. But the woman flees into the wilderness which here is understood, as in the Exodus story, as a place of safety and freedom. The church, too, then, is protected by God and cannot be destroyed even by persecution.

The passage can be related to Mary as the one who is the representative of the church. The good news is that the evil—the idolatries—of our society, including perhaps even evil within the church itself, cannot possibly overthrow the work of God. God, through "the authority of his Christ," will judge evil and redeem his church.

SECOND LESSON

Lutheran and Episcopal: Gal. 4:4–7. This passage occurs in the context of Paul's discussion of slavery under the law and of Christian freedom. The contrast is between being a slave and being a son. The change of status comes about through an event, the sending of God's Son, and is confirmed by the gift of the Spirit which enables the believer to address God as Father.

The movement of thought in this passage is clear. It begins with the affirmation that we are all "under the law." We are in need of redemption. To be "under the law" is to be a slave. We are under a constant demand to prove ourselves worthy, to establish our status and dignity. Slaves are of no value to their masters except for what they can do. When we conceive our situation before God as "under the law" we too are in the same situation. We must prove our worth.

The preacher needs to reflect on what it is that functions as "law" in our society. How does one find status and dignity? Perhaps it is in our work where the "law" is the demands of the boss or the corporation and we remain enslaved in obedience to them because not to do so would rob us of our sense of worth. Perhaps the "law" is the demands of the family, or self-imposed demands which appear to sum up what it means to be a worthwhile person.

Whatever the particular form of our enslavement, the lesson speaks of God's act which sets us free. "When the time had fully come, God sent forth his Son, born of woman, born under the law." The first part of this verse, is more literally translated, "when the fulness of time had come." The word "fulness" means the "content of an event which sums up the meaning of a long period of time." Christ's coming brought to fulfillment the events which preceded it. God "sent him forth." The word here is related to the word "apostle." Christ is God's Apostle who entered completely into the reality of human life. He was born of woman like all human beings and he was born under the law. The last phrase means, of course, that he was a Jew but it also means that he entered into the sphere of human life with its inevitable threat of enslavement.

Paul's reference here is not explicitly to Mary, and it does not really speak to the issue of the virgin birth. It does, however, speak about how God has exalted Mary by choosing her as the mother of our Lord, and by the gift of grace which enabled her to accept that role.

The purpose of Christ's coming was to "redeem those who were under the law, so that we might receive adoption as sons." The word "redeem" means to buy back, and is associated with buying the freedom of a slave or a prisoner. Through God's power this purpose is carried out. We are set free, and the mark of that freedom is our new status. We are adopted as children of God. The word adoption is a legal term. It means that a person is made a member of a new family and given the rights and privileges of that membership, including in particular the right of inheritance. The term is used by Paul in somewhat different ways. It refers in Rom. 9:4 to the special relationship between Israel and God, and in Rom. 8:23 it refers to the eschatological hope for which Christians wait. In this passage it refers to the new status Christian believers have as a result of Christ's redemption. These ideas are all related. Because of our new status we now share in the gift of God to Israel, although the fullness of that gift is yet to come.

Our new status as "children" means that we are free from slavery to the law. Our status and dignity do not depend on what we do but rather on God's acceptance of us. Unlike slaves, children are valued by their parents not for what they do but for what they are. Paul's affirmation is that through the redemption that Christ brings we are adopted and given a new status. We are free therefore from the slavery of having to establish our worth by obedience to some law. We no longer have to prove that we are better than somebody else in order to show that we really count for something.

Because we have this new status, "God has sent the spirit of his Son into our hearts, crying 'Abba! Father!' " "Spirit" is a word which means "breath" and is therefore associated with life and with the power to express oneself in words. Because of God's act we are now the recipients of the spirit of Christ. We live by the power which he gives us, a power which is marked by our new ability to address God as Father. The word *Abba* is the Aramaic word for father, the word a child would use to address his father in an intimate and affectionate way. The good news of the gospel is that we can now address God in that way. We are free as children to express our new relationship in the most intimate way. The Book of Common Prayer puts it this way: "We are bold to say, Our Father . . ."

This new relationship to God means that we no longer need to live in fear. We need no longer worry about whether we will be acceptable like an employee who constantly worries about whether he or she can please the boss. We are now a part of the family with an assured place and with the certainty of our inheritance. "You are no longer a slave but a son, and if a son then an heir."

Mary serves as an example of the persons of faith. She is enabled by

es, and he has sent the rich away empty." The language here is
"revolutionary." It expresses the biblical bias in favor of the poor.
t its deepest level it expresses the paradox of God's action. His final
r us appears not as an act of power but of humiliation. He comes as
y and he dies on a cross. The mystery of the gospel is that that
g and that cross are more powerful than any thing else in the
, for they are the power of God's love.

hymn ends with the affirmation that the coming of Christ is the
ent of the promises to Israel. Mary is the representative of that
. She is one of the "poor ones," that is, one of the pious and
Israelites who can now rejoice that God has fulfilled his prom-
ary thus can be a symbol of the church, of the new people of God
t into being by God's gift of himself in the person of Christ. The
ael is called to sing the praises of the God who has brought us
nce from our humiliation and freedom to live as children of God.

St. Bartholomew, Apostle

AUGUST 24

Lutheran	Roman Catholic	Episcopal
Exod. 19:1–6		
		Deut. 18:15–18
1 Cor. 12:27–31a	Rev. 21:9–14	1 Cor. 4:9–15
John 1:43–51	John 1:45–51	Luke 22:24–30

mew is named in the synoptic Gospels as one of the twelve
osen by Jesus, but very little is known about him beyond that
church tradition says that he was a missionary to various
cluding India and gives various accounts of his death. The
olomew is a patronymic, meaning "son of Tolmai." Because
here has been much speculation that Bartholomew also had
e as did Simon Bar-Jona. Since Bartholomew's name fol-
in the lists of disciples in the Gospels (though not in Acts),
ilip is closely associated in John's Gospel with Nathanael,
n a tendency in the Christian tradition to identify Barthol-
athanael. The former appears only in the synoptics and the
John. This identification explains the use of the Gospel
John in the Lutheran and Roman Catholic lectionaries for
reading in all the lectionaries tends to focus on the meaning
and its relation to the church rather than on Bartholomew
al.

the grace of God to accept her role and to trust in the God who gives her a
new status.

SECOND LESSON

Roman Catholic: 1 Cor. 15:20–26. This reading continues to focus on
resurrection, as did the first reading. It is an appropriate theme for this
day in the Roman Catholic tradition, which celebrates the Feast of
Assumption. The passage occurs in the midst of Paul's defense of the
resurrection as a future reality for Christians, a truth which the Corinthians, with an over-realized eschatology, wished to deny.

The movement of Paul's argument is clear. He begins with the facts of
Christ's resurrection. He has already shown that to deny it is to undermine the Christian faith. In any case, "Christ has been raised from the
dead." That fact has been attested by the tradition he has cited above
and by the witnesses he names. The important point here is that that
resurrection is "the first fruits of those who have fallen asleep." The
image comes from the OT and the requirement that the first part of the
harvest be given as a thank offering and as a sign assuring the rest of the
harvest. Christ's resurrection therefore assures the resurrection of
all believers. Even more important, Christ's resurrection inaugurates
the new age. "For as in Adam all die, so also in Christ shall all be
made alive."

The thought in this last sentence involves the idea of a representative
person. Adam represents humanity in solidarity with its enslavement to
sin and death. To be alive is to live always in the presence of the anxiety
of death. We know that there was a time when we were not and that there
will be a time when we will be no more. Such knowledge drives us to try
to make ourselves immortal by what we do. We struggle to achieve
power and mastery over life. We want to be like God. Alternatively, the
fear of death can paralyze us so that we are afraid to enter into another
life. We play our cards "close to the chest" for fear that to risk new
relationships or enter new situations may destroy the tenuous hold that
we have on our own dignity and worth. It may in that sense "kill"
us. The good news is that we are not only "in Adam" but we are also
"in Christ."

"In Christ" we have the assurance that death is not the end but that it
leads to new life. We can dare and risk because of that assurance and
because we know that not even death itself can overcome the power of
God's love.

There is, however, an order to be observed. First, Christ. Then, at the
Second Coming, "those who belong to Christ." Only then will come the
end of history and the establishment of God's kingdom with its final
destruction of "every rule and every authority and power" including the

last enemy, death itself. Paul's argument here is that the resurrection is an assurance of victory, but that the final victory is eschatological. In this world the struggle against evil always goes on albeit in the light of the assurance of final victory.

Paul's words about order suggest that the resurrection is future for all except Christ himself. Mary's participation in the new life must be understood in the light of her participation "in Christ." She is the forerunner of "those who belong to Christ." She may be taken to represent the whole church as we struggle against evil and endure the anxiety of death, in the assurance of final victory given by the One who for our sake "became incarnate from the Virgin Mary."

GOSPEL

Lutheran, Roman Catholic, and Episcopal: Luke 1:46–55. This passage is Mary's hymn of praise to God, commonly known as the Magnificat. It is Mary's response to the blessing given to her by Elizabeth and to Elizabeth's report that the child in her womb "leaped for joy" when Mary came and greeted her. (The Roman Catholic lectionary includes the account of Mary's visit to Elizabeth which begins in verse 39.) The main theme of Mary's hymn is praise to God for his faithfulness and the fulfillment of his promises, such as those mentioned in previous readings. That fulfillment reverses what appears to be the normal order of human life. The hymn contains echoes of the language used to describe the Exodus, the great saving event of the OT (Exod. 15:1–8), and also reflects the hymn of praise spoken by Hannah at the birth of Samuel (1 Sam. 2:1–10).

The hymn begins with Mary's declaration of praise. The words "my soul" and "my spirit" really mean "I" or perhaps, "I with all my being." Mary "magnifies" the Lord; she "declares his greatness" and rejoices that the Lord is the one who saves. The word "rejoices" is a very strong one and means "to exult, to rejoice exceedingly," and it is used in the NT to speak of the joy that accompanies the fulfillment of God's promises. The term "savior" is often used in the OT to apply to God and it means that he is the one who rescues his people from oppression and gives wholeness and fulfillment to their lives.

The movement of the hymn becomes obvious in v. 48. Mary describes herself as one who has been in "low estate." The word here means "humiliation" and it is used in the Septuagint to refer to barrenness, but the word also has a much broader meaning. Since Mary is speaking in this passage as a representative of Israel, the humiliation referred to here clearly means Israel's humiliation at the hands of the Romans. The "low estate" is the condition of those who are oppressed and who are looking

for deliverance and vindication. The question for th
understand the low estate of those to whom he
Perhaps for some it is the humiliation and oppressi
brought on by a real or imagined failure to measure
family or society. For others it may be the oppress
which tempts one to think that life is about the que
a view which constantly threatens to undermine
it may also be "slavery to the law," as discuss

The turning point in this situation is that C
"regarded"—that is, turned his attention with
low estate of his handmaiden." The hymn now
reflects the Exodus story in the OT. "God has
last two words are used in Deut. 10:21 and
describe the Exodus. The reference to "showi
is also an echo of Exodus language. The po
which Mary finds herself is the time of fulfi
deliverance, a new freedom. The forthcom
God's holiness. "Holy is his name." The wo
apart." It points to the otherness but also to
which manifests itself in faithfulness and j

"His mercy is on those who fear him.'
Greek word used to translate the Hebre
steadfast love of God who remains faithfu
then sees the coming of the Christ as the m
ness to his covenant. He does not aban
them—and to us—in mercy. The coming
tion for it is the final proof of the love, ca
of all appearances to the contrary, we ar
This Gospel, indeed, *the* Gospel, affirm
and the will to be a savior, to enter
oppression, evil, and death, and to be

This mercy of God is on "those who
the response of fear, fear in the sense
of the Holy One. God's action produc
way contrary to human expectations
human life. "He has scattered the
hearts." The "proud" are those w
others, who give the appearance of
status before God depends not on
has done for us, there can be no
come from those who have worldly
mighty (the Greek word can me

FIRST LESSON

Lutheran: Exod. 19:1–6. The setting of this passage is in the wilderness near Mount Sinai. Israel has already passed through the Red Sea, and it is now the beginning of the third month since that event. Moses has brought the people to the mountain to which God had bidden them come, and has himself gone up the mountain to talk with the Lord.

The Lord's words have a threefold structure. First, they speak about the past. "Thus shall you say to the house of Jacob, and tell the people of Israel: 'You have seen what I did to the Egyptians, and how I bore you on eagles' wings and brought you to myself.'" The story begins with what God has done. He has rescued his people from slavery to the Egyptians and brought them safely to himself. The eagle is an image which suggests a bird that trains and supports its young; so God has supported his new people. The important point is that Israel's life is grounded in the Exodus, in God's saving act which gave the people their freedom, indeed their very existence.

The second stage is the present consequence of this past act. "Now therefore, if you will obey my voice and keep my covenant, you shall be my own possession among all peoples; for all the earth is mine." The result of the Exodus is that Israel has the possibility of a new status. If the nation accepts the covenant which God offers, it will be his own possession. Israel has a special status among all the nations of the world. It has been chosen by God, to whom the whole earth belongs, by an act of his sovereign freedom.

The third stage is the future implications of this election. "You shall be to me a kingdom of priests and a holy nation." To be chosen by God is to be called as a people to be a priestly nation, that is, to be the nation which mediates between God and human beings. Israel is holy, set apart, as a sign that all people belong to God. It is called to be a priestly people, to be the bearer of God's word to the world.

As the preacher reflects on this passage on this day, he or she may wish to think of Bartholomew the apostle as a representative of the church. We, like Israel, find our identity as a people in an event in the past. The Exodus gave Israel freedom from slavery in Egypt. The cross and resurrection, which are at the heart of the apostolic witness, gave us freedom from the slavery of sin—that is, the need to show that we are worthy of God's love and concern, or the equally serious problem of being certain that we are beyond all doubt totally unworthy and therefore without hope. We are also set free from the fear and anxiety of death, for the resurrection is the assurance of the triumph of God's love even over death.

The past event then means that as a people we have a new status. We are God's possession. Our identity as a church is a gift of God, who acts out of sheer grace. The whole world is his and yet he chooses to call a particular people. The fact that we celebrate the life of a particular man about whom we know very little symbolizes the particularity of God's call to us as a church to belong to him. Here the preacher needs to be very careful. The call of the church is not a form of elitism, for that call is for the sake of the world. Like Israel we are called to be a priestly people, a nation set apart, "in the world but not of the world," a nation called to bring the word of God's love to all. An apostle is always "sent" on a mission. The preacher may wish to consider the ways in which the apostolic calling and sending on a mission is reflected and expressed in the life of the particular parish he or she is serving.

SECOND LESSON

Lutheran: 1 Cor. 12:27–31a. This lesson is the end of the chapter in which Paul has been speaking of the church as the body of Christ. The emphasis is on the diversity of gifts which are given to individuals, a diversity which serves the well-being of the whole, with renewed emphasis on the church. This passage is appropriate for this day since it stresses the primacy of the apostles. Bartholomew as an apostle symbolizes the apostolic witness which establishes the church and in the light of which the church always continues to live. "God has appointed in the church first apostles, . . ." Just as in the Exodus passage Israel has "seen what I did to the Egyptians. . . ." so the church always looks back to what God has done in Christ. That backward look is possible only because of the apostolic witness to the cross and resurrection. But there are other gifts as well. Some are prophets—those who interpret God's judging and redeeming word to the particular concerns of the moment. Some are teachers or healers. Others are helpers—those who give succor and support to the poor, the helpless, and the needy. Others have the gift of speaking in tongues or of interpreting tongues.

The point is that since our status before God depends on what he has done in Christ, then we are free to accept these other gifts knowing that we too are part of the body. This passage gives the preacher an opportunity to reflect on how the Gospel sets us free to serve others. The apostolic witness which Bartholomew symbolizes is the good news of our acceptance and new status with God. The apostolic example includes the example of service to others. How is the apostolic witness expressed in our parish and how does that witness enable us to enter into the apostolic example, to receive and affirm and use the gifts that we have been given?

SECOND LESSON

Roman Catholic: Rev. 21:9–14. The emphasis in this passage is also
on the church and on its apostolic foundation. The seer receives a
message from an angel and is taken up to a "great high mountain" to see
the "Bride, the wife of the Lamb." The Bride is, of course, the church,
the messianic people whom the Messiah claims as his own. The mountain is an idealized Mount Zion, where the new city of God will be. There
are two important points in the passage. The first is that the author sees
"the holy city Jerusalem coming down out of heaven from God." The
church is a gift of God, not a human creation.

The preacher may wish to reflect on the fact that community is, in the
last analysis, a gift and not something that we make for ourselves. When
we focus on "community" it tends to evaporate. The church has its
common life not because people gather together to make a new community, but because the church is the creation and gift of God which comes
down from heaven.

That leads to the second point. The foundation of this new community
is the apostles themselves. The church exists because of the apostolic
witness and it is a community because we all share in the common life
created by that witness. The life of the church is nourished and
strengthened by hearing again the apostolic witness to the cross and
resurrection. In that way the church, like the heavenly Jerusalem, has
"the glory of God."

GOSPEL

Lutheran and Roman Catholic: John 1:43–51. The Gospel is the call
of Nathanael who, as mentioned above, is often identified with Bartholomew. Even if the identification is incorrect the story still is an appropriate one for it really sets forth a kind of ideal apostleship. Jesus' call to
Philip is "Follow me." Philip is summoned to leave Bethsaida and go
with Jesus; to encounter Christ is to encounter the one who asks you to
leave the familiar and come out on a new journey. He not only asks that,
but he makes it possible. To encounter Christ is to be given a new way of
looking at the world. Love is greater than hatred and life is stronger than
death. That new way of seeing the world means that we are able to do
new things, to journey in a new direction, to take risks that otherwise
would be impossible. It also means that like Philip we are eager to call
others.

"Philip found Nathanael." Philip's words to Nathanael meet with an
initial negative response. "Can anything good come out of Nazareth?"
Not very complimentary to the reputation of Nazareth! Yet these words

express the difficulty which we all have and which indeed all the disciples had. It is very difficult to believe that a particular human being from an insignificant little village should be the means of God's final revelation to all the world. Nathanael responds as any of us might do. But he does "come and see."

Jesus' words begin the process of changing Nathanael. "Behold, an Israelite indeed, in whom is no guile." Unlike Jacob, this Israelite will not receive his new status by trickery (guile), but as his name, Nathanael, indicates, as a gift of God. Before Philip called him, Jesus saw him "under the fig tree." The latter phrase is the OT description of an ideal Israelite. Jesus' insight into who he was convinces Nathanael, and he confesses Christ. What attracts Nathanael is what attracts us all. In the words of Christ we find ourselves. He knows who and what we are. His teaching exposes the reality of human life in its brokenness and its need for fulfillment. "He speaks with authority." Nathanael confesses Christ to be "the king of Israel."

Yet that is not the final apostolic witness. Nathanael, who represents the true Israel, the new people of God called into being and given the gift of life by God himself, has yet more to see. "You will see heaven opened, and the angels of God ascending and descending upon the Son of man." The true and final apostolic testimony is not that Jesus is the king of Israel, but that he is the one who links heaven and earth. Not Jacob's ladder but Christ himself is the means of access to heaven. That is possible only through the cross. Nathanael, like the other apostles, will see the cross which is the final revelation of the judgment and the love of God. It is to that that the apostles bear witness, for they alone know the meaning of the cross since they alone are the witnesses of the resurrection.

The Nathanael story reminds us that the good news of Christ overcomes our reluctance to know him. The preacher may reflect on the things in our culture which are barriers to hearing the message of the gospel. How then does the witness of the apostles, of Bartholomew and the others, break through that reluctance and enable us to see the "angels of God ascending and descending upon the Son of man"?

FIRST LESSON

Episcopal: Deut. 18:15–18. The theme of this reading is the promise that the Lord will raise up a new prophet like Moses. It is in the context of a passage about the need for Israel to avoid the heathen practices of the land into which it is coming and instead to obey the commands of the Lord. As the need arises, God will send a prophet to interpret those words. As Christians we see the fulfillment of this prophecy in the coming of Christ.

On this day we think especially of the apostles as the ones who bear witness to that fulfillment in Christ. Bartholomew and the others are the bearers of the Lord's word to us as we too live in a strange land. The preacher may wish to reflect on how the practices and the standards of our world, the many "gods" which we worship, pose a threat to our hearing the apostolic message. The lessons which follow seem to build on this theme, for they suggest that the standards of this world are dangerous indeed. The Corinthians thought that the genuineness of apostles was measured by their ability to do miracles rather than their ability to share in the suffering of Christ. The disciples in the Gospel also want to share in the kingly rule of Christ, and they dispute who is the greatest.

Does the church today, does one's own parish, wish to hear the apostolic witness or does it find its norms and standards in the surrounding culture? How are we to be freed to receive that witness? The lesson suggests that we do not do it on our own, but that like the Israelites we need a gift of God's grace. The good news of this day is that the witness of ordinary people like Bartholomew to the truth of the Gospel can set us free.

SECOND LESSON

Episcopal: 1 Cor. 4:9–15. The Corinthians apparently held a Gnostic-like view of the Christian faith which emphasized that the Kingdom of God was already present. "Already you are filled!" Paul says with biting sarcasm in the verse which precedes this passage. He then goes on to show the true nature of apostleship. We are "last of all," "like men sentenced to death," "a spectacle to the world," "fools for Christ." He writes this, he says, "not to make you ashamed," but as a "father in Christ Jesus through the gospel." The point of his words is that the apostles reflect in themselves the center of the gospel, which is that God has brought new life out of death and that there is meaning in suffering, for it participates in the redemptive suffering of Christ. Success for the church is measured by its participation in the gospel message, by its hearing the good news that we are free to accept whatever happens in the world because we are secure in the love and power of the Christ who died and rose again.

The preacher should reflect on the life of the church today. Does it participate in the example offered by Paul and the apostles or are we more like the Corinthians, looking to affirm that we already have arrived? To raise that question is not to seek to shame the church but to call it always to look to the Christ who gave us life and is the true Father of this new community.

GOSPEL

Episcopal: Luke 22:24–30. The same themes found in the earlier lessons are present here. The apostles prove that they are all-too-human by arguing over who is the greatest among them. Jesus' word to them is that they are trying to live by the standards of the culture which surrounds them; "the kings of the Gentiles" do this sort of thing. For the apostles the measure of greatness is to be the measure of service. They have Christ himself as the example for that. But even more the good news of the Gospel is that we are free to serve, for our status does not depend on what we do but on what God has done for us in Christ.

The woman in the advertisement who doesn't "do windows" holds to that position as a way of affirming her dignity. The apostles too thought that they should have a certain dignity which went with their position. And indeed they do. The Lord tells them that they will judge the twelve tribes of Israel. But that position is theirs because they have continued with Christ in his trials. They have stayed with Christ and have come to know that the cross is the means that God uses to assure us of his love and power. We are given the gift of life and status; and therefore we are free to serve, just as the apostles who once argued over greatness became free to serve.

The feast of an apostle gives us a chance to reflect on the meaning of the apostolic witness and example. How do we as the church live out our gospel freedom to serve others?

Holy Cross Day
(Roman Catholic: Triumph of the Cross)
SEPTEMBER 14

Lutheran	Roman Catholic	Episcopal
Isa. 45:21–25	Num. 21:4–9	Isa. 45:21–25
1 Cor. 1:18–24	Phil. 2:6–11	Phil. 2:5–11 or Gal. 6:14–18
John 12:20–33	John 3:13–17	John 12:31–36a

This day is associated with the dedication of the church built by the emperor Constantine on the traditional site of the crucifixion. The Church of the Holy Sepulchre now occupies the site to which Christian pilgrims have journeyed for centuries. The lessons for this day invite the preacher to reflect on the meaning of the cross of Christ, the very center of the Christian faith, and encourage us to celebrate the victorious power of the cross. The day provides an opportunity to preach on the cross in a mood different from the solemnities of Lent and Good Friday.

FIRST LESSON

Lutheran and Episcopal: Isa. 45:21-25. The broad context of this passage is the prophecy of Second Isaiah at the time of the Exile with its promise of restoration and hope. The cross is thus seen in the light of the judgment and renewal represented by that great moment in Israel's history. Since a dominant theme in Second Isaiah's work is the universality of God's power, the cross is seen also as the means of God's inclusion of all nations in the saving power of Christ.

The specific context of this passage lies with an oracle that speaks of the final judgment on the idolatry of the nations. Looking back over history God invites the nations to "present your case." The language is that of the courtroom. A trial is in progress. The witnesses—the "survivors of the nations" (v. 20)—are asked to testify. "Who told this long ago? Who declared it of old?" That is, who is the one who told of the judgment that was to come? The answer could only be the Lord. "There is no other god besides me." That is the final word of judgment on the idolatry of the nations. Idolatry involves the elevation of some aspect of creation into a position of lordship over creation. The ancients tended to try to make the processes of nature, the cycle of the seasons, seedtime and harvest, into gods. Today we are perhaps more likely to do it with economic interpretations of history or nationalism or even internationalism. Individualism, especially in its "me first" form, is another example. "It is all right to spend this money on myself because *I* am worth it." The preacher needs to reflect on the current forms of idolatry which dominate our world.

Whatever forms the idolatry may take, it always comes under the judgment of the biblical witness to the one God who, as Isaiah states, is "a righteous God and a Savior." These words are crucial to an understanding of this passage and of the cross. The word "righteous" means not only that God is right and just, but also that he acts to make things right. He vindicates and delivers those who are oppressed. It is no accident that the word paired with "righteous" is "savior." These terms are not opposites but complementary, indeed virtually synonymous. God is righteous because he is a savior.

The events of the Exile have established God's righteousness. Israel has been judged for its idolatry. The problem with idolatry is that it makes a god out of something which has no moral power at all, like the cycle of nature, and thereby robs human life of any meaning. Life is literally then "just one damned thing after another." Or it can elevate something which is too narrow to be the basis of ultimate judgment, such as nationalism. Only the Lord of history himself can be the proper basis for providing meaning and judgment in life.

But even more important, the Exile has shown that God acts to put things right, to save. Israel will be restored and there will be a time of fulfillment. No idol can do that. The Lord's salvation means that there is hope in human life. Without forgiveness and restoration there is only the possibility of enslavement, an enslavement to a moralism in which there is no room for forgiveness. But the Lord is a righteous God and a Savior. The two themes of judgment and salvation sounded here in Isaiah come to their fulfillment in the cross. There the Christian finds the ultimate expression of the righteousness of God, a righteousness which condemns sin and also acts to overcome it with the power of love and forgiveness.

The Isaiah passage then takes up the call to "all the ends of the earth" to turn to God and be saved. The verb "turn" implies facing and looking in a new direction. Since the Lord is the only one who has the key to the meaning of history, the only source of true prophecy, then he alone can be the source of life and salvation. This insight invites us to reflect on what we turn to for life, hope, and salvation. Is it perhaps an idol—something other than God? Do we not sometimes at least try to find salvation in our own abilities to cope with the complexities of life? If we immerse ourselves in our jobs, or our relationships, or in the pursuit of the good life, all will be well. We turn to such things to be saved.

But now we read that the Word has gone forth. God has sworn by himself. "Word" means not only what God says but also what he does. Thus the Exile is part of the word of the Lord as is also, preeminently, the cross. His word will not "return." That is, it will not turn and start off in a new direction nor will it be taken back. Hence that word can be trusted. And that word is for everyone. "To me every knee shall bow, every tongue shall swear."

The prophecy ends by reiterating that the Lord alone is the source of "righteousness and strength." The latter word means the power to accomplish what one wishes. It can refer to physical strength or political power. Here it clearly means God's power to accomplish his objective, and implies contrast with the weakness, indeed helplessness, of the idols. The irony is that the strength of God will be displayed most forcefully in the same cross which appears to be utter weakness. The strength of God is the power of sacrificial love. This understanding is foreshadowed in this passage by the fact that the nations which were "incensed" against the Lord, that is, were hot with anger, will come to him and be ashamed. The Lord does not blot out the nations that have been guilty of idolatry but shames and humbles them with the power of forgiveness. Because "triumph" (the Hebrew word is really "righteousness," the victorious vindicating power of God) and "glory" (which means the gift of eschatological fulfillment, a restoration of the status that Adam had) are "in the Lord," they are now available to all. The "offspring of Israel" is now potentially everyone who accepts the Lord's gift.

FIRST LESSON

Roman Catholic: Num. 21:4–9. Instead of focusing on the Exile, this passage focuses on the events of Israel's wandering in the wilderness. It is used as a metaphor for the cross in the Gospel of John. While the story may have its roots in primitive ideas of demons in the wilderness and in the power of sympathetic magic, the central thrust of the passage is toward the biblical themes of sin, judgment, and redemption.

The Israelites have met opposition in their attempt to enter the land of Canaan and so they set out to go around the land of Edom, a longer way to their goal. The people "become impatient." The Hebrew word here means that their spirit became short. They were at the end of their rope. They were discouraged. They protested against God and against Moses. In typical human fashion they also blamed the food. It was "worthless." The Hebrew word means "slight, trifling, of no account, not substantial." The food, which was the gift of God, did not seem sufficient to the Israelites to sustain them. The sin of the Israelites then was their despair, their refusal to trust in the power of God to take them forward, and their desire to turn back to Egypt.

The preacher will wish to reflect on the ways in which we lose patience in our situation. We find fault with the "food" which the Lord offers us in life. Life is too complex in our world. If only we could go back to a simpler society where moral choices were clearer. Is it really possible to endure the pain and suffering which seem to be our lot?

The judgment of the Lord comes on them in the form of "fiery serpents." The Hebrew word for "fiery" is *seraphim* and presumably refers to the inflammation caused by the serpents' bite. The serpents bite the people and many die. The good news is that this judgment produces a change in the people. They recognize their sin in that they had "spoken against the Lord" and against Moses, and they ask Moses to pray that God will take away the serpents.

Their prayer is answered, but not exactly in the way that they had asked. The serpents are not removed, but Moses is instructed to make an image of a serpent and place it on a pole. Whenever anyone is bitten, that person is to look at the serpent and "he shall live." The judgment is not removed, but a means of redemption is offered. The serpent no longer has the power to kill, but while still being the vehicle of God's judgment, it also becomes a means of freedom and life. The lesson gives us an opportunity to reflect on the cross as the vehicle of God's judgment which is also the means of redemption and life. The cross does not remove human pain and suffering but it allows us to see them in a new way. In the light of the cross we see that pain and suffering cannot destroy life ultimately; indeed if we can learn to understand our suffering as a participation in Christ's afflictions (Col. 1:24), we will be pointed to the sacrificial love of God which is victorious and life-giving.

SECOND LESSON

Lutheran: 1 Cor. 1:18–24. This passage picks up from the Isaiah passage the theme of the promise of salvation and the revelation of the power of God, but the fulfillment of the promise takes a quite unexpected form. The "word of the cross" is Paul's summary of the basic message of the Christian faith. The central point is the crucifixion seen as God's redemptive act. The cross can be seen, however, from two different points of view. "The cross is folly to those who are perishing." To those who insist on having life on their terms and who are therefore being destroyed the cross is folly. A foolish person is one who is imprudent, who makes no reasonable provision for the future. From the world's perspective, the cross is that kind of foolishness. It speaks of total self-giving which keeps nothing back, and it runs counter to the obvious evidence of the world that the only way to accomplish anything is to have power and control, to have "the biggest legions."

To us who are being saved, however, the cross is the power of God. The word "power" also means "a mighty act." The cross is the mighty act of God. What it does is to turn things upside down. As Isaiah had predicted (29:14), God has destroyed "the wisdom of the wise." Paul plays on the word "wisdom" throughout this passage. It can mean on the one hand "human wisdom." In Greek, the word *sophia* referred to the wisdom of philosophy, the power of human reason to penetrate the inmost meaning of the world and life. This idea may be in the background of this passage, but Paul seems mainly to be thinking of the "wisdom" or "knowledge" that was characteristic of gnostic thought. Those who held gnostic views thought that they held the secret of who God really is and that they understood and were assured of the place of human life in the cosmos. This view elevates not God but humanity. *Our* knowledge and *our* wisdom become the source of life and salvation.

But wisdom also means the true wisdom of God, which is expressed in the cross. The cross is the means whereby God, in *his* wisdom, invites and enables us to believe, to trust that in spite of all the appearances to the contrary at the very heart of the world there stands the unshakeable power of the sacrificial love of God. "In the wisdom of God, the world did not know God through wisdom." The ultimate truth did not come through human wisdom; neither the philosophical speculations of the Greeks nor the constructions of *gnosis* were able to help us see this ultimate truth. Truth came only through the "folly of what we preach," and it has the power "to save those who believe." The word "save" suggests health, wholeness, fulfillment of life. It is for Paul an eschatological term. The final goal of human life and of human history is salvation.

It is worth noting that Paul speaks of both Greeks and Jews. "Jews demand signs and Greeks seek wisdom." Paul's point is that this desire for signs is a denial of the cross. The demand for signs is the desire to have a tangible assurance of the power of God, a miracle that will establish the certainty of God's control. Like the search for wisdom, it too is an approach to the problem from the human side, a search for assurance on our own terms.

The preacher needs to reflect on the ways in which our culture seeks wisdom and demands signs. Do we believe that the key to the meaning of human life is to be found in ever more sophisticated forms of research, physical, psychological, or historical? In our religious lives is there sometimes a tendency to demand signs, to think that the Christian faith can be validated only when it provides answers to the problems that *we* have formulated? Do we want assurance that faith works because we can see it meeting our immediate needs?

The Christ whom Paul preaches is a "stumbling block to the Jews." That is, he is a cause of offense, a provocation to sin for those who demand tangible assurance. Historically the belief in the crucified Messiah seemed an incompatible one to Jews who believed that the very essence of messiahship was victory over Israel's enemies. And the cross is still a stumbling block to such human expectations and assumptions. How can one win by losing? Then too, to the Greeks the cross seems incongruous. How can something which so clearly denies the power and value of human reason and undermines the quest for that which affirms the divine spark in humanity be of God?

"But to those who are called"—to those who in the mysterious working of God's providence are chosen—to them "Christ (is) the power of God and the wisdom of God."

SECOND LESSON

Roman Catholic and Episcopal: Phil. 2:5–11. This passage occurs in the midst of Paul's plea for unity in the church and is intended as an example to the Philippians. The passage is a christological hymn which sets forth in poetic form the drama of salvation.

Although Christ was "in the form of God, (he) did not count equality with God a thing to be grasped." The word "form" implies not the appearance of something, but a shape which is totally consistent with the inner reality of that thing. Christ then is pictured as being one with God. But he did not regard that divine status as something to which he must cling as booty which had been seized. Instead he "emptied himself, taking the form of a servant." Christ's act was one of self-giving in which he entered into the reality of human life."He humbled himself and became obedient unto death, even death on a cross."

This description of Christ reflects the idea of Christ as the new Adam. Adam too was in the likeness of God but he *did* count equality with God a thing to be grasped. The serpent tempted Adam to eat the fruit of the tree of knowledge saying that he would then be like God. The punishing result of Adam's disobedience was expulsion from the garden. He lost the status which he had had. The result of Christ's act of obedience was that God "highly exalted him and bestowed on him the name which is above every name." A name reveals the true character of the one who possesses it. The name which Christ now has been given is the name "Lord," the very name of God himself. Because he has that name, "every knee should bow, in heaven and on earth and under the earth." Christ's coming and death have revealed the true nature of God and also the true nature of humanity. He is therefore the fulfillment of the promises of Isaiah and the source of universal salvation.

The passage invites us to reflect on numerous themes. The hymn presents a vivid picture of the divine condescension in coming to us and accepting the fullness of the human situation even to death. It stresses the centrality of self-giving love. The relationship of the hymn to the story of Adam enables us to see that the true meaning of human life is to be found in obedience and submission to the will of God. We are tempted to assume that the fulfillment of life consists in having power, in being like God. The hymn reveals that true lordship comes through giving oneself, "even to death." "For whoever would save his life will lose it; and whoever loses his life for my sake and the gospel's will save it." The cross is not a means of humiliation but of exaltation, for it represents the ultimate point of Christ's obedience to God, an obedience which both provides us with an example of true human life and incorporates us into the new humanity. It frees us to begin to enter into that example.

GOSPEL

Lutheran: John 12:20–33 and Episcopal: John 12:31–36a. The Lutheran Gospel has three parts. It begins with the request of the Greeks to see Jesus, moves to Jesus' response to the request, and ends with the Johannine form of the agony of Christ which includes an interpretation of the meaning of the cross.

The opening section, the request of the Greeks to see Jesus, is, as it were, an account of the apostolic mission of the church in reverse. The apostles took the message of the gospel out into the gentile world after the death and resurrection of Christ. Here the Greeks representing the Gentiles come to Philip, a disciple with a Greek name who comes from Bethsaida, a city with many Gentiles, and ask to see Jesus. He tells Andrew, and together they go to Jesus. Instead of the apostles going to the Gentiles, the Gentiles come to them. The Greeks wish to see Jesus, that is they wish to see the one whose name means "the Lord saves." The Greeks are seeking salvation.

The coming of the Greeks provides the preacher with an opportunity to reflect on the need of the world for salvation. Why does anyone want to see Jesus? Is it not because there is something missing in life? Is there not some need, conscious or unconscious, to see the One who can save? To be a Gentile meant to be outside the covenant community, outside the community whose lives were given meaning and purpose by the call to be obedient to the law of God and who were sustained by the continuing steadfast love of God. As the Isaiah passage showed us, Israel knew the Lord to be "a righteous God and a Savior." Now the Gentiles too come to see the one who claims to fulfill the promises of the prophets.

The second element in the passage is the response of Jesus. It is an interesting response in a typically Johannine form. Jesus does not really respond to the request directly. He does not refuse to see the Greeks, but he does not see them either. (John is here reflecting the fact that the historical Jesus' ministry was virtually exclusively among Jews.) Instead, Jesus takes the discussion to a new level. "The hour has come for the Son of man to be glorified." The "hour" in John's Gospel refers frequently to the time of Jesus' death, and it certainly does so here. In addition, Jesus' "glorification" takes place on the cross, for it is there that Jesus makes his final act of obedience to the Father and thereby offers praise (glory) to God and is in turn the recipient of the glorification which comes from God. Christ is glorified by his death in that the cross is the means by which God acts to show the depth of his love. In the Isaiah passage God's glory is revealed in the return of Israel from Exile and in the promise that all the nations will come to acknowledge him as Lord. Now that promise is being fulfilled. The true power of God is revealed in the sacrificial love of Christ. A seed does not bear fruit unless it dies, that is, rots away in the ground. The analogy here is that the seed of the gospel too requires a death before there can be fruit. The mission of the church is possible only after the cross.

The Gospel gives the opportunity to reflect on the cross as the means which enables us to find life by losing it. John sees the cross as a symbol of victory, of glorification. As servants we too are called to follow Christ. The good news is that such a following which involves self-sacrifice is the way to find life. Since the cross is the center of God's revelation and since, like the seed, death brings forth fruit, then sacrificial self-giving is the means to new life. The preacher's task is to help others see how the word of the cross speaks to a culture in which acquisition and consumption are the virtues, and where the mark of glorification is the size of the paycheck ,or status in the hierarchy of business or professional life.

In the third section we see John's picture of Jesus' struggle with the reality of the cross. His "soul," that is, his inner being, is troubled. He cannot ask to be saved from "this hour" because it embodies the very purpose of his coming. Indeed the call to the disciples to follow Christ is impossible apart from his own death. Christ's prayer is "Father, glorify thy name." The prayer asks God to reveal in a decisive way his nature and his power. The answer is that the Lord has done this already, and that he will do it again. He has done it in creation and in the history of Israel. The Exodus and the Exile were glorifications of God's name. Now he will do it again. These words of God have come, we are told, for the sake of those who are witnessing these events. They need to know the meaning of the cross.

In the climax of the passage that meaning is expressed. "Now is the judgment of this world, now shall the ruler of this world be cast out." The cross is the moment of judgment. The cross reveals once and for all the depth of human sin and at the same moment overcomes it. A physical analogy is, just as the availability of food can make us aware of how hungry we are, so to in a far more profound sense does the cross reveal the seriousness of sin even as it breaks the power of that sin. "The ruler of this world will be cast out." The ultimate threat of the power of sin is that if we do not yield to it, we will die. Christ robs sin of that power by accepting the threat. "Go ahead and kill me," is what Christ is saying.

The power of sin is broken by that acceptance and thereby the universal meaning of the cross is revealed. "I, when I am lifted up from the earth, will draw all men to myself." The phrase "lifted up" in John refers both to the physical lifting up on the cross as well as to the exaltation to heaven. The cross is the means whereby Christ is exalted because it is the means whereby we can know who he truly is. His death is a victorious act of love with the power to draw all people to him. The victories of God in the OT—the Exodus and the Exile—foreshadow the cross. They can be understood as victories on behalf of a particular nation. But the cross is universal, for it addresses the universal human problems of sin and forgiveness, of death and new life. As the passage goes on to say, Christ fulfills the promises but in an unexpected way. He does remain forever, but not as the military leader of a nation. He remains forever as the "light" which enables us to become children of light.

GOSPEL

Roman Catholic: John 3:13–17. This Gospel returns to the story of the serpents in the wilderness. It comes at the end of the discourse with Nicodemus in which the topic is the possibility of new birth and new life.

This new life is available only through the Christ, for "No one has ascended into heaven but he who descended from heaven, the Son of man." There is no link between this world and ultimate reality except Christ, the Son of man. And the link through Christ is possible only by way of the cross. "And as Moses lifted up the serpent in the wilderness, so must the Son of man be lifted up." The term "to lift up" in John has a double meaning. It refers to the physical "lifting up" of Jesus on the cross. But it refers also to the exaltation of Christ, to his being lifted up to heaven. In other words John is saying that the crucifixion of Christ is also his exaltation to heaven. The cross is at one and the same time the revelation of who Christ truly is and his ultimate act for us and our salvation. Like the serpent in the wilderness, the cross is both judgment and salvation. The cross reveals the depth of human sin and also overcomes it so that "whoever believes in him may have eternal life."

All this is possible because the cross reveals the ultimate intention of God, which is love. "God so loved the world that he gave his only Son." The passage invites us to reflect on the meaning of the cross as the expression of the love of God. The cross, like the serpents in the wilderness, involves the judgment of God. Only in the light of the revelation in Christ culminating in the cross can we understand fully the meaning of God's holiness. True love, as opposed to sentimentality, is not without judgment. But though the cross brings judgment, it does not bring condemnation. "For God sent the Son into the world, not to condemn the world, but that the world might be saved through him." This verse expresses the purpose of God and because it is God's purpose it cannot fail. The result of Christ's coming is, therefore, salvation.

The connection of this Gospel with the reading from Numbers invites reflection on the meaning of the cross as both the judgment and the love of God. The preacher may wish to reflect on the way in which love, perhaps love of a parent for a child, may express itself in judgment, while also reflecting on the fact that such love always has as its aim not condemnation but redemption. Such love works by evoking a response from the one who is loved and produces, as its corollary, trust or faith on the part of the loved one.

St. Matthew, Apostle and Evangelist

SEPTEMBER 21

Lutheran	Roman Catholic	Episcopal
Ezek. 2:8—3:11		Prov. 3:1–6
Eph. 2:4–10	Eph. 4:1–4, 11–13	2 Tim. 3:14–17
Matt. 9:9–13	Matt. 9:9–13	Matt. 9:9–13

GOSPEL

Lutheran, Roman Catholic, and Episcopal: Matt. 9:9–13. The one verse, v. 9, about Matthew is all the NT tells us about him. He was a tax collector who was called by, and then followed, Jesus as a disciple. The verse is set in the context of Jesus' forgiving sinners and eating with sinners.

"As Jesus passed on from there (that is, "his own city" in which he had demonstrated his God-given authority to forgive by forgiving and healing a person who had been paralyzed), he saw (*"to become acquainted with by experience; to care for"*) a man called Matthew sitting at the tax office (*"toll-house*: the place in which the tax-collector sat to collect taxes") and he said to him, 'Follow ("[prop. walking the same road] *to cleave steadfastly to one, conform wholly to his example,* in living and if need be in dying also") me.' And he rose and followed him."

What did Matthew do as a follower of Christ? Ancient testimony and some modern scholarship ascribe all or part of the First Gospel to him. If that is so, a study of the First Gospel is a study of the tax collector's later theology.

There are traditions which hold that Matthew was a missionary, first among the Jewish people and later among the Gentiles. Some say that he died as an old man, others as a martyr by burning. But of none of this can we be certain.

It is widely accepted that Matthew is the same person as Levi the tax collector in Mark and Luke. If so, following the Lucan parallel, the rest of the story takes place in Matthew's house.

"And as he (Jesus) sat at table in the house, behold many tax collectors and sinners came and sat down with Jesus and his disciples." ("The *tax collectors* were, as a class, detested not only by the Jews but by other nations also, both on account of their employment and of the harshness, greed, and deception with which they prosecuted it. *Sinners* were those who 'miss the mark'; acc. to Pharisees, all persons not as punctilious as they. The *disciples*, in a wide sense, in the Gospels, those among the Jews who favored Jesus, joined his party, became his adherents; but especially the twelve apostles.")

What kind of gathering was this? It might be compared to a pastor and a group of loyal parishioners meeting with a group of persons who are social outsiders or outcasts. Whatever the agenda, the meeting itself would offend some people, as the Pharisees were offended by this scene.

"And when the Pharisees saw this, they said to his disciples, 'Why does your teacher eat with tax collectors and sinners?'" (*Pharisees*: "sought for distinction and praise by the observance of external rites and by outward forms of piety, such as ablutions, fasting, prayers, and alms-giving; and comparatively negligent of genuine piety, they prided themselves on their fancied good works." Many houses were such that the Pharisees could see and talk into the eating rooms from the street. *Teacher*: "in the NT one who teaches concerning the things of God, and the duties of man.")

The Pharisees could not imagine a legitimate "why" for what Jesus was doing. According to their calculations, what Jesus was doing was flagrantly wrong. Jesus' eating with tax collectors and sinners would establish and signify a bond of fellowship between them and him. These were people who, to the Pharisees, were "unclean" and should be ostracized. It would be virtually impossible for even the most conscientious tax collector to remain "clean." The job involved touching "unclean" persons (for example, unclean by virtue of being a Gentile or of having neglected to do the "ablutions, fastings, prayers, and alms-giving" which the Pharisees demanded) and touching "unclean" coins (unclean by virtue of having an image of Caesar stamped on them). The "sinners" could have been other persons who because of their occupations, lack of money, or lack of time did not keep the rules of tithing or ritual bathing.

The sinners and even the much-maligned tax collectors eating with Jesus were not necessarily willful or malevolent people. They represented a hefty majority of Israel who were unable or unwilling to live by the complex, time-consuming, and costly punctilios for maintaining the status of "clean."

Nevertheless, persons designated "unclean" or "sinners" according to the pharisaic rules were not allowed to attend synagogue. Certainly, according to the Pharisees, no genuine teacher of Israel would eat with such persons. So their question "Why?" may have carried a tone of incredulity as well as condemnation.

Jesus heard the Pharisee's question, and he answered, "Those who are (in their own eyes) well (a metaphor for righteous) have (they think) no need of a physician (that is, an agent to make them well or righteous), but those who are sick (that is, those whose need for the wholeness which Jesus offers is manifest)."

Then, Jesus concluded his reply with an admonition, "Go and learn what this means, 'I desire mercy ("readiness to help those in trouble"), and not sacrifice (that is, religious practices).' For I came not to call ("to make the offer of salvation by the Messiah") the righteous ("those who seem to themselves to be righteous, who pride themselves on their virtues, whether real or imaginary"), but sinners (such as those with whom Jesus was eating)."

One might enter this story as Levi (and his fellow tax collectors and sinners) before he was transformed into Matthew the disciple (or as Matthew who sometimes loses faith in the gospel and falls back into his old way of life). One who is like Levi sins against the economic, social, or religious values of his own society. This kind of sin may reveal a lack of love for one's neighbor. It often results in a lowering of self-esteem incurred by the criticism and condemnation of one's peers. Whatever the specifics of this type of sin, it is overt and patently "bad," and a "Levi" can hardly avoid awareness of his or her need for Jesus' wholeness, just as the tax collectors and sinners in the Gospel had an awareness of that need.

One might also enter the story as a Pharisee. A Pharisee punctiliously upholds the values which he, as a religious or social authority, deems "good," but he is so intent on his own goodness that he may fail to love others, and he despises those who hold different values. As Jesus described them, such Pharisees are like a "whitewashed tomb." There is a kind of "beauty" in the outward goodness of this scrupulosity, but inside the "tomb" is full of the bones of those killed by this lovelessness and of the uncleanness of calculating self-righteousness.

In what ways are you, the preacher, a Levi or a Pharisee?

Are you a Levi aware of your "sickness": of your unworthiness, of your loneliness, of your rejection, of your guilt? If so, what does Jesus say to you (and the Levis in your congregation) which might make you more well and thus enable you to follow him more closely?

Are you a Pharisee self-consciously and calculatingly trying to achieve and claim your rightness? Are you so hungry for "distinction and praise" that you disdain and avoid those who do not contribute to your success? If so, what does Jesus say to you (and to the Pharisees in your congregation) which might give you the rightness, the distinction, or the praise you seek and free you from pharisaic pretensions?

These are two ways one might enter this story. In either way, the movement of the meditation and the sermon might be toward a greater "health" which enables closer discipleship. We now turn to the other readings for further clues to guide the meditative application.

SECOND LESSON

Lutheran: Eph. 2:4–10. This reading offers many clues for applying the Gospel's movement from being a Levi or a Pharisee to being a disciple like Matthew. This reading also abounds in gospel content, to raise a Levi to a sense of self-esteem or to remove a Pharisee from self-righteousness.

Either as a Levi or as a Pharisee, we are "dead" (*"destitute of a life that recognizes and is devoted to God"* [and the gospel and people of God]) through (better "in") our trespasses (*"a lapse or deviation from truth and uprightness"* i.e., the truth of the gospel and the uprightness it effects)." Levis are "dead" from the weight of their failings, because they are ignorant of the truth of God's mercy and love (v. 4) and the rightness he imputes. Thus they are "dead" also to the potential "good works" (v. 10) of spontaneous and uncalculating love. Both the Levi and the Pharisee in us need the truth of God's gospel which this reading contains.

First, even while "dead in our trespasses," God has "loved us" with a "great love" ("the benevolence which God in providing salvation for men, has exhibited by sending his Son to them and giving him up to death").

Second, because of his "great love," God is "rich in mercy ("esp. the mercy and clemency of God in providing and offering . . . salvation in Christ")."

Third, all this is "by grace" ("that kindness by which God bestows favors even upon the ill-deserving, and grants to sinners the pardon of their offences"). That is, it is sheer gift from God and is not based on our works (achievements or accomplishments, whether internal feelings or external activities).

The gospel of this "grace"—the mercy of God which springs from his great love for us—engenders the faith which saves us from being "dead." There are three images for this salvation in the reading:

(1) God "makes us alive" (*"a life active and vigorous, devoted to God, blessed, the portion even in this world of those who put their trust in Christ"*).

(2) God "raises us up" ("from moral death to a new and blessed life devoted to God"). He makes us sit (live) with him in a heavenly existence in Christ Jesus (and his gospel). Then, as the successive segments of our lifetime pass, he shows us the transcendent riches of his graciousness in kindness (or mercy, opposite to severity in Rom. 11:22) toward us in Jesus Christ.

(3) God "creates" us (forms or transforms us), by uniting us with him "in Christ Jesus" through the gospel which proclaims him. Thus created, we can "walk in" (do) the life-enhancing "good works" which "God prepares beforehand" ("in mind and purpose") in con-

trast to the death-dealing "trespasses" which we prepare in our
minds for a self-serving purpose.

We have no grounds for boasting about salvation in any of the above
forms, for none of them is our achievement nor do we merit any of them.
They are all gifts of God, even the desire to do good works. The
self-esteem which acknowledged sinners like Levi need has been im-
planted by the gospel of the love and mercy of God who raises us to sit
with him in the heavenly throne room. The pseudo-self-esteem which
the Pharisee in us tries to grasp is replaced by the esteem in which God
holds us by grace. Out of the richness of God's love and mercy, knowing
we have been given seats with him in heaven, knowing that we are made
righteous and esteemed by God, we can do good works without the
hidden agenda of gaining self-righteousness or self-esteem.

FIRST LESSON

Lutheran: Ezek. 2:8—3:11. This reading is packed with material
about preaching. The difficulty of preaching is vividly portrayed and the
reading, along with its context, affirms the ground of confidence in the
urgency and effectiveness of preaching. But to focus on the lesson from
that perspective would lead us away from the perspective set by the
Gospel and the Second Lesson. Seen from this perspective, it provides
further clues for the movement from being a Levi or a Pharisee to a
Matthew "saved by grace through faith."

In this reading, the "house of Israel" was found, to use the phrase
from Ephesians, "dead in its trespasses"; or, to use Jesus' term, it was
"sick." But Israel was unaware of its condition. The house of Israel was
"of a hard (*"strong* [usu. in the bad sense, *hard, bold, violent*]")
forehead (as the *"open* and *prominent"* expression of self)." It was also
"of a stubborn (*"severe* [in various applications]:—churlish, cruel,
grievous, hard, stiff, stubborn") heart ("the *heart*, also used [fig.] very
widely for the feelings, the will and even the intellect; likewise the *centre*
of anything")."

God gave Ezekiel words designed to make the house of Israel aware of
the sickness and deadness of its heart and its concomitant actions. They
were "words of lamentation ("a *dirge* [as accompanied by *beating* the
breasts or on instruments]") and mourning ("a *muttering* [in sighing,
thought, or as thunder]") and woe ("wailing")." They were the kind of
words said or sung over the sick and the dead. When the house of Israel
heard such words it could no longer deny its condition.

In what follows this lesson the meaning and purpose of the above
words is made more explicit. These words said to the wicked mean
"You shall surely die ("lit. or fig.")." The purpose of these words is to
"warn" ("to *gleam*; fig. to *enlighten* [by caution]") the wicked (for

example, a Levi or a Pharisee) "in order to save his life" ("to *revive* life, whether lit. or fig.") so that the "wicked" shall not die in their "iniquity" (twisted out of shape).

As a Levi or a Pharisee, what sickness or deadness, what hard forehead or stubborn heart, do you see in yourself or in others which evokes words of lamentation, mourning, or woe? How might a deeper faith in the great love and rich mercy of God toward you, as exemplified by Jesus' coming to eat with you, affect this condition?

SECOND LESSON

Roman Catholic: Eph. 4:1–4, 11–13. While the Gospel calls us from being Levis or Pharisees to being Matthews, this reading gives characteristics of this calling.

First, a Matthew is characterized by "lowliness." This means literally "not rising far from the ground." As a metaphor, it means having "a deep sense of one's (moral) littleness," a down-to-earth person, not stuck-up. It is a derogatory label outside the NT. But when one is secure in the high status and imputed righteousness graciously given by God, there is no need for self-elevation or for self-righteousness. If you know you've *really* got it (that is, status and righteousness from God through Christ), you don't need to flaunt it. The parallel term "meekness" refers to virtually this same characteristic.

Second, a Matthew is characterized by a "patience" which manifests itself in "forbearing one another in love" and being "eager to maintain the unity of the Spirit in the bond of peace." This "patience" means literally a long temper in contrast to a short temper. As a Levi or Pharisee we are short-tempered because we are insecure about our status, our righteousness, and our future. But as Matthews, who have heard the gracious and merciful call of Christ to be his, we are secure in the status, righteousness, and future which he gives us. In Christ, one is not subject to the short temper of insecurity. One enjoys the long temper of the security of belonging to "one Lord, one faith, one Baptism, one God and Father of us all."

SECOND LESSON

Episcopal: 2 Tim. 3:14–17. The thrust of this lesson is toward being a "Matthew," that is, toward being "the man (or woman) of God . . . complete, equipped for every good work." The message which effects the transformation from being a Levi or a Pharisee to being a Matthew is alluded to but without content. For the sermon to be effective, the preacher needs to fill in the content of "what you have learned and . . . believed" from the "sacred writings."

As you identify some aspect of your life as a Levi or a Pharisee, what is the message that transforms you into more of a Matthew? What is the gospel content?

FIRST LESSON

Episcopal: Prov. 3:1–6. In this lesson we are provided with further material for portraying a Matthew in contrast to a Levi or a Pharisee.

Matthews do not forget God's teaching (*torah*), but their hearts ("the feelings, the will and even the intellect") keep God's commandments in active memory.

Matthews do not rely on or lean on themselves, but trust the Lord and turn to him to "make straight" ("fig. to *make right, pleasant, prosperous*") their paths in life.

Matthews understand God's commandments primarily as his gracious acts on behalf of his people. Matthews understand God's *torah* primarily as the story of "all the saving deeds of the Lord which he performed for you and for your fathers." Matthews are grasped by the "loyalty and faithfulness" of this God toward his people and therefore answer his call to be his.

In contrast, Levis forget God's teachings and commandments and act only for themselves, oblivious to what God desires of them. Pharisees distort teachings and commandments into rules by which they try to create themselves and their way in life and so claim the credit. Pharisees rely on themselves rather than trust in God for selfhood.

St. Michael and All Angels
(Roman Catholic: Michael, Gabriel, and Raphael)
SEPTEMBER 29

Lutheran	Roman Catholic	Episcopal
Dan. 10:10–14, 20–21	Dan. 7:9–10, 13–14 or Rev. 12:7–12	Gen. 28:10–17
Rev. 12:7–12		Rev. 12:7–12
Luke 10:17–20	John 1:47–51	John 1:47–51

FIRST AND SECOND LESSONS

Roman Catholic, Lutheran, and Episcopal: Rev. 12:7–12. What happens in heaven results in "fallout" consequences on earth. What happens on earth is grounded in heaven. Also, derivatively, what happens on earth affects heaven so there is two-way communication between earth and heaven. The Primary Initiative is the heavenly. Variously called First Cause, Ultimate Sovereignty, Divine Providence, or God, it is the Giver of the given in the givenness of life. The secondary initiatives of us earthlings in history are not only derived from the Primary Initiative but are fed into the cosmic system (or story) and by God's mercy used to serve the purpose of the God who is King over heaven and earth. This interplay between heaven and earth has been called "the cosmology of the Apocalypse."

For us earthlings, this cosmology means that we are not victims of amoral and impersonal fate or chance. The evil powers of Satan do not rule history. We are not controlled by the inexorable and uncaring movement of the stars. Neither movements of history nor the coincidence of circumstances have the "last word." The throne room of the cosmos is in heaven and the heavenly Cause of causes and King of kings is personal, benevolent, and purposeful.

In this cosmology, when we earthlings cry out to heaven, whether in gratitude or complaint, we address a personal God and the lesser persons in the heavenly court; we are assured of a benevolent basic intent in the throne room; and we are promised that earthly history serves a heavenly purpose. The enduring significance of the earthly is revealed in the heavenly.

In this passage war has occurred in heaven. Already there had been two heavenly signs which interpreted earthly events in terms of heaven. First, there was a woman, whose twelve-starred crown showed her to be the fullness of mother church who comprehends the essential oneness of the twelve tribes of the old Israel and the twelve of the new. Through the suffering of mother church, Christ (and new life in him) has, does, and will, come into the earthly realm.

Opposing the woman was a second sign: a great dragon who sought to devour the woman's child at birth and thus destroy Christ and preclude the church. But, when Christ was born as the ruler of all peoples, God defeated the dragon, for the "child was caught up to God and to his throne" (in the resurrection-ascension). Mother church fled to the place God had prepared for her in the wilderness (the time between the decisive victory and its final consummation as in the Exodus). There the church would be sustained for three and a half years, a number symbolic of the evil time which results when the seven-day week is broken, the in-between time in which the defeated dragon would be desperately fighting its last.

This sequence of heavenly decisive victory which spelled eventual victory on earth, followed by an in-between time of intense suffering, concluded with a consummation of the victory. This is what is portrayed in today's lesson. First there is the dragon, the destroyer, and his angels, the representatives of his power. The dragon is identified with the "serpent" of Gen. 3:1 and is characterized as "ancient" or "properly, that which has been from the beginning, original." The dragon is also called the "Devil" (false accuser) who slanders God's people before God in an attempt to alienate the King from his subjects. Another name for the dragon is "Satan," that is, the "adversary" who opposes God in purpose and in act. He is described as "the deceiver of the whole world," for he attempts to lead God's people away from faith into apostasy.

Supporting the woman and opposing the dragon and his angels were Michael and his angels who, phenomenologically, are representative of God's power and, semantically, metaphors for God's power. God defeated the dragon by the war in heaven and correlatively by the crucifixion and resurrection of Christ on earth. The dragon and his angels were thrown out of the heavenly throne room. No longer did they have access to the King of kings through the heavenly court. The dragon, alias serpent, alias Devil, alias Satan, was decisively defeated. Heaven proclaimed the victory of God and the servants of God over the evil dragon and all his powers:

> This is the hour of victory for our God,
> the hour of his sovereignty and power,
> when his Christ comes to his rightful rule!
> (NEB)

The defeat of the dragon was initiated in heaven. It was an act of "divine initiative." It was an act of God.

The defeat of the dragon was and will be historically actualized on earth. Derivatively, the historical actualization is human activity, the acts of real women and men. "They (sisters and brothers to Christ) have conquered him (the dragon) by the blood of the Lamb (the crucifixion-resurrection analogue of the victory in heaven)."

What marvelous irony! A lamb, an *arnion,* small and weak by worldly calculations, a metaphor for both Christ and his flock; in the amazing economy of God the *arnion* defeats the *thērion,* the beast. Christ and his flock turn out to be lions in lamb's clothing (Rev. 5:5–6).

When the lesson takes on a theological perspective, it is by the blood of the Lamb, which is the power of God, that faithful men and women conquer the dragon. From an anthropological perspective, the dragon is conquered first by the power of human words of witness to "the salvation and the power and the kingdom of . . . God and the authority of his Christ" and second, by the fact that through the promise of their witness, the faithful are made willing to suffer and die with the Lamb and for his sake. The willingness of Christians to suffer and die nullifies the power of the dragon over them. In his attempts to lead the faithful into apostasy, the worst threats the dragon can mount are suffering and death. But to the faithful the threats of suffering and death are ineffective because they have already been "willing to give up their lives and die" (TEV).

So heaven rejoices and those who dwell in heaven (in fact or by faith) rejoice. But calamity will yet befall earth and sea for the devil-dragon has come down in heated, desperate anger because he knows that only "a short time (in which to exercise his power) has been granted him." This is the in-between time which suffers the insanely destructive rage of evil powers who know they are defeated.

The consummation of victory comes later. The dragon is seized and finally annihilated. In the meantime, on earth, Christians are enabled to resist apostasy and to remain steadfast in faith and works by their witness to the heavenly promise of the end time.

Before considering clues for meditating on this passage, a brief excursus on angels and eschatology. As suggested earlier, the term "angel" or "messenger" functions, phenomenologically, as the thrust of the power of the one who acts and, semantically, as a metaphor of that power. One's action and its impact can be expressed metaphorically as a sender sending a message to another. For example, someone does an action to another and asks, "Did you get the 'message'?" The receiver replies, "Yes, I got the 'message'." So the actions of power of God, Satan, and human beings can be represented metaphorically as angels.

We have managed to write what we have without resorting to the term eschatology even though it has been the central topic. Basically, eschatology has to do with who or what has the "last word" (the eschatos-logos) and the content of that word. In today's lesson there is no question that it is God, not Satan, who has this "last word" both in the meantime and at the end of history. God's word is a word of sovereign authority and power. History is primarily *His Story* and only derivatively the human story.

Meditation on the reading might then be focused on who you believe has the last word and on its content. Does God or Satan have the last word? Whose is the authority, power, and victory in your life, in the lives of people you know, in the life of the nation? Does it sometimes seem that it is the destructive dragon, the tempting serpent, the false accuser, Satan the adversary and deceiver of the whole world? Does evil seem to be defeating good? If so, how does this affect behavior? How do you feel? How do you act? Does it lead to apostasy from faith or works as it did with some members of the Seven Churches? Does this reading renew faith in God as the last word? Does the significant role of humans in the defeat of the dragon affirm significance for what you do? What is the content of God's last word as found in this and other readings? What do these words and images say to you? What might they say to your congregation?

We turn now to the other readings for further material for meditative reflection, guided by this lesson which is central to the feast and common to all three lectionaries. The other readings contain visions of heaven and angels and each suggests a complementary nuance of meaning.

FIRST LESSON

Lutheran: Dan. 10:10–14, 20–21 and Roman Catholic: Dan. 7:9–10, 13–14. Daniel, like Revelation, portrays both heaven and earth and their interplay. Chaps. 1—6 tell about earthly events, especially about Daniel and his faithful friends. The scene is Babylon during the Exile in the early part of the sixth century B.C. The literary form is prose. The underlying theme is God's greatness.

Chap. 7 begins the climactic heavenly visions which bring the theme of God's greatness and the interplay of heaven and earth onto center stage. The literary form of the visions shifts from prose to poetry. Chronologically these visions could be sandwiched into the first part of the book as heavenly theological analogues of the earthly anthropological events.

In a dream, Daniel had a vision which, as the image of the four winds and other uses of the number four suggest, comprehends the whole of earthly history. The dream or vision occurred at night when it was dark on earth. The vision of vv. 1–8 portrays four terrifyingly malevolent, powerful, and destructive beasts. The four beasts are interpreted as kings or kingdoms (Dan. 7:17, 23). They might be thought of as earthly powers which seek inordinate dominion and which threaten well-being. Such powers terrorize the earth and cover its people with a pall of darkness.

Beyond terror and darkness, Daniel saw a vision of thrones, the symbols of power, but all the thrones were vacant except one. Only "one that was ancient of days" (that is, one who was old) was seated on his throne. None of the beasts was seated on its throne, for they had all been dethroned. The worst of the beasts had been slain. The others, although without dominion, were allowed to live a limited time longer (v. 12). Earthly existence and power is perceived as derivating from the heavenly here and in v. 6.

In v. 13, it is still dark on earth, but now the ancient one on his throne is recognized as God (thus the RSV's capitalization of "Ancient of Days"). To God the Ancient of Days "came one like a son of man" with the clouds of heaven—a symbol of the interplay between heaven (God) and earth (humanity). The Ancient of Days gave to the one who came an everlasting dominion/kingdom that shall not pass away or be destroyed.

To be "like a son of man" is literally to be like a man or a human being, an *anthropos*. Ezekiel is addressed as "son of man." But, in the symbolic and charged context of this vision, the reader is inclined to ask with the Psalmist, "What is man . . . the son of man?" Who is this one to whom God gives everlasting authority and dominion?

The parallels in 7:14, 18, and 27 argue that the "one like a son of man" is representative or first fruit "of the people of the saints of the Most High." The one like a son of man has been identified with the Messiah in both Judaism and Christianity and with Jesus as the Messiah in Christianity. The portrayals of the "one like a son of man" in Dan. 7:13 and Rev. 1:13 and "the man" in Dan. 10:5 overlap and seem to refer to one figure who, in Revelation, is clearly Jesus risen and ascended in victory.

Thus the central good news which this feast proclaims is that, in spite of all earthly appearances to the contrary, the victorious power of "everlasting dominion" resides in Jesus, whom God the Father, "Ancient of Days," has raised up to reign as God the Son over the whole of heaven and earth. And through Jesus (as son and husband of the woman in Revelation), a community of disciples is formed as "the people of the saints of the Most High" to share the blessings of victory.

As with the brethren or believers and disciples in the Second Lesson, "the people of the saints of the Most High" have suffered and will suffer on earth for three and a half time periods, that is, an evil but limited broken sabbatical time (Dan. 7:21, 25). But the eschatology, the last word, is certain. All power and dominion is given by God and exists only at his pleasure. In heaven, beastly powers have been dethroned. It is only God, the Ancient of Days, who is enthroned. The other thrones are empty. It is only the One who appears human, the representative of humanity and the first fruit of "the people of the saints of the Most High" who has been granted "everlasting dominion (or power)."

History is not ended. The saints will endure further suffering and death, but remember—Jesus applied the "Son of man" title to himself in the context of earthly suffering and death (Mark 8:31). Yet later, in the context of his victorious coming in majesty, Jesus used the name again (Mark 14:62). Through this Jesus we and all his saints "shall receive the kingdom, and possess the kingdom for ever, for ever and ever" (Dan. 7:18).

Primarily, on the heavenly-theological level, the power and the victory are God's doing. Derivatively, on the anthropological-earthly level, the power and the victory are the doing of humanity. The two levels are interlaced into one story, and the eternal significance of the human enterprise is affirmed by its being raised up and incorporated into the divine (cf. 12:3).

All that has been said about Daniel so far serves as background for the

reading from Dan. 10:10–14, 20–21 in the Lutheran lectionary. What
follows also provides further context for the Roman Catholic reading.

The vision recounted in this passage happened on the twenty-fourth
day of the first month, right after Passover and the Feast of Unleavened
Bread, when past deliverance in the Exodus had been commemorated
and future deliverance had been anticipated, so the religious situation
was ripe for a vision of deliverance. In the vision, a man, who through
the eyes of Christian faith (as previously suggested) might be identified
with the Lord Jesus appeared to Daniel. (See similar imagery in Rev.
1:12–17; 2:18.) His companions fled, leaving Daniel alone, his strength
drained, "a sorry figure of a man" (NEB), flat on his face.

As the reading begins, the power of the man's touch brings Daniel up
on his hands and knees. The power of the man's words then brings
Daniel up on his feet, albeit still trembling.

"Fear not, Daniel," the man said, "for from the first day that you set
(or "gave") your mind ("the feelings, the will and even the intellect") to
understand and humbled yourself (kept yourself down-to-earth) before
your God, your words have been heard (in the heavenly council through
your angel), and I have come because of your words."

The vision seems to assume a heavenly council composed of angels
(or princes) who represented residents of earth, both individual and
corporate, before the King of kings. The prince-angel who represented
Persia withstood "the man" in the heavenly council for a time, but
Michael, one of the chief princes (who represented Israel) joined forces
with "the man." This freed "the man" from heavenly council duties so
he could bring his message concerning the future to Daniel to enable
Daniel to stand up and assume dominion.

In the omitted vv. 15–19, Daniel fell flat on his face again, but again
"the man" raised him up by his touch and words of hope.

Then "the man" told Daniel two things about the content of God's last
word. First, the warfare with evil will continue for a time both in heaven
and on earth. When "the man" returns to heaven, he will have to fight
against the prince-angel who represents Persia and, that done, against
the prince-angel who represents Greece (two enemies of the old Israel
and symbols of enemies of the new). Only the prince-angel Michael, who
represents Daniel and all the servants of God, stands with "the man" in
the heavenly conflict as on earth only his servants stand with him.
Conversely, "the man" had stood up "to confirm and strengthen"
Michael (and through Michael, Daniel and all "the people of the saints of
the Most High").

Second, "the man" told Daniel "what is inscribed in the book of
truth" about warfare in the earthly sector. This message comprises
chap. 11 of Daniel. "The man's" message to Daniel is epitomized in the

eschatological last word of 12:1–3, which summarizes the great gospel affirmation of the feast. "There shall be a time of trouble" (in fact, many times), such as there never has been before. But "at that time shall arise Michael, the great prince (angel) who has charge of your people (the servants of God)." "At that time your people shall be delivered, every one whose name shall be found written in the book (of the living). And many (or, more likely, all) of those who sleep in the dust of the earth shall awake, some to everlasting life, and some to shame and everlasting contempt. And those who are wise shall shine like the brightness of the firmament. . . ."

In spite of all evil powers, in spite of suffering and death, the final truth is that the "wise" will be resurrected to "everlasting life." Who are the wise? In the book of Daniel they are those who, as recipients of "wisdom and understanding" given to them by God via Gabriel (9:22), are *enabled* by God to know God and to serve him by resisting evil. For us, today, the wise are those who, as recipients of wisdom and understanding given to them by God via the Gabriels of today's Scripture and you the preacher, are *enabled* to know God and to serve him by resisting evil and striving for good.

In reflecting on either reading from Daniel, the preacher might identify evil powers (internal or external to us) which we are called to resist. Do you (and your congregation) tend to fall down passively in fear or hopelessness and quit the battle? What last word good news is there in the lessons about God's powerful and victorious sovereignty over evil which might enable you or your congregation to stand up and fight the good fight? What last word good news is there about God's present caring and concerned listening to us via the angels who represent us in heaven? What last word good news is there about the everlasting significance of our words and actions as they are raised up and incorporated into the working out of God's heavenly purpose? As God's "angel" in this liturgy, what good news can you bring from heaven to enable "the people of the saints of the Most High" to remain firm in faith and works?

GOSPEL

Lutheran: Luke 10:17–20. Here the Gospel gives a glimpse of the heavenly visions which were recounted more fully in the Revelation and Daniel passages, more explicitly in the former. Satan has been cast out from heaven. Therefore, derivatively on earth, demons (Satanic angels) are subject to disciples of Jesus in his name. His name carries the full authority and power of God over the adversary. Jesus is thus identified with "the man" the "one like a son of man," of Daniel and Revelation.

V. 20 asserts the primary significance of the things we say and do in the name of Jesus, the primary ground for rejoicing in our various ministries. The primary significance of what we say and do is not grounded in earthly results as such. The primary significance is grounded on the promise that we humans and what we say and do are signified or written in heaven. The disciples were getting highly successful results in their ministry. "Nevertheless," Jesus told them, "do not rejoice in this, that the spirits are subject to you; but rejoice that your names are written in heaven."

Meditation on this reading might well follow the suggestions given in the two previous sections. The passage affirms good news about the power and significance of what we say and do as our ministries are mercifully raised up and incorporated into God's purpose which by his power will be accomplished.

GOSPEL

Roman Catholic and Episcopal: John 1:47–51. The Fourth Gospel is concerned with "seeing" coupled with where and what one sees. In this Gospel Nathanael was so impressed with Jesus' earthly seeing that he responded with a confession of faith in Jesus as "Son of God" and "King of Israel." Jesus' reply did not demean earthly seeing, but he pointed to a "greater" more significant seeing—the earthly coupled with the heavenly as in the angels ascending and descending. This interplay between the heavenly initiative and the earthly derivative is also found in the Genesis reading considered below. The angels of God communicate the earthly words and deeds of the Son of man (individually and corporately as his church) to God, and they communicate God's word power (especially personified by Gabriel) and action power (especially personified by Michael) to earth.

Suggestions for reflecting on what we see on earth and on the relationship and significance of the earthly (humanity) in its interplay with the heavenly (God) are found in the comments on Revelation and Daniel above.

FIRST LESSON

Episcopal: Gen. 28:10–17. The section on the Daniel readings should be read as background and guidance for reflection on this passage. In the Daniel section, we saw angels as expressions of the interplay between heaven (God) and earth (humanity). In that interplay, angels represent humanity before God in the heavenly council, and angels represent God's word and action on earth. The Genesis reading portrays this two-way interplay and something of the content of God's word and action. Meditative reflection on the reading might well use the suggestions given in the sections on Revelation and Daniel.